THE FRONT LINES OF SOCIAL CHANGE

THE FRONT LINES OF SOCIAL CHANGE

VETERANS OF THE ABRAHAM LINCOLN BRIGADE

RICHARD BERMACK
FOREWORD BY PETER N. CARROLL

HEYDAY BOOKS, BERKELEY, CALIFORNIA

This book is dedicated
to the three thousand
Americans who joined the
forty thousand volunteers from
all over the world to risk their
lives fighting in Spain for the
rights of others.

"Two Americas," from *Exorcising Terror: The Incredible, Neverending Trial of Augusto Pinochet,* © 2002 by Ariel Dorfman, reprinted with the author's permission. "The Carpenter Swam to Spain" © 2005 by Martín Espada, reprinted with the author's permission. Rosario Pistone's recollections from *Premature Antifascists* ©1986 by John Gerassi, reprinted with the author's permission. "Passport Not Valid for Travel in Spain" by Mike Quin reprinted with permission of International Publishers. "But What about the Guys in the Lincoln Brigade" © 2005 by John Sayles, reprinted with the author's permission.

Library of Congress Cataloging in Publication Data:
Bermack, Richard.
  The front lines of social change : Veterans of the Abraham Lincoln Brigade / Richard Bermack ; foreword by Peter N. Carroll.
    p. cm.
  ISBN 1-59714-000-7 (pbk. : alk. paper)
  1. Spain–History–Civil War, 1936-1939–Participation, American. 2. Spain. Ejército Popular de la República. Abraham Lincoln Battalion. 3. Americans–Spain–History–20th century. 4. Soldiers–Spain–Attitudes. 5. Americans–Spain–Attitudes. 6. Veterans of the Abraham Lincoln Brigade. 7. Spain–History–Civil War, 1936-1939–Veterans. 8. Veterans–United States–History–20th century. 9. Social movements–United States–History–20th century. 10. Veterans–United States–Attitudes. I. Title.
  DP269.47.A46B47 2005
  303.48'4'092273–dc22

                                                                    2004021497

Book design by Rebecca LeGates
On the cover: Marching in San Francisco against the first Gulf War, c. 1990: Milt Wolff, Clifton Amsbury (in back), Al Tanz, Ted Veltfort, and Lenore Veltfort.

Orders, inquiries, and correspondence should be addressed to:
  Heyday Books
  P.O. Box 9145, Berkeley, CA 94709
  (510) 549-3564; Fax (510) 549-1889
  www.heydaybooks.com

Printing by: McNaughton & Gunn, Saline, MI

10 9 8 7 6 5 4 3 2 1

CONTENTS

"I've never been part of a cause that won, but I still feel like the richest man in the world."

—Abe Osheroff, Abraham Lincoln Brigade veteran

"I did what I could to create a more equal world."

—Sana Goldblatt, founder of the San Francisco Bay Area Veterans of the Abraham Lincoln Brigade

"You have to get in the good fight and stay in it. Life is pointless unless you have a moral or ethical outlook. I don't care what channel, whether you're a communist or a Quaker, as long as that is the aim—to alleviate hunger in Ethiopia, or stop the war in Iraq, Afghanistan, Nicaragua, or El Salvador, or end the U.S. blockade of Cuba. It's not Spain by itself, but the whole thing, that is the good fight."

—Milt Wolff, the last commander of the Abraham Lincoln Brigade

LIST OF PHOTOGRAPHS

ACKNOWLEDGMENTS

I would like to thank the following: Peter Carroll, Marge Lasky, and Louis Segal for reading earlier versions of the manuscript and providing insightful and helpful critiques; Julia Newman of the Abraham Lincoln Brigade Archives, Mark Rosenzweig at the Peoples Weekly World Reference Center for Marxist Studies, Erika Gottfried and Michael Nash at the New York University Tamiment Library, and Cary Nelson for help with the historical images used in the book; Judy Montell for use of the transcripts from her films *Forever Activists* and *Professional Revolutionary: The Life of Saul Wellman;* Peter Glazer for his advice, support, and encouragement; and Jeannine Gendar, Rebecca LeGates, Patricia Wakida, and Malcolm Margolin at Heyday Books, whose expertise and faith in the project made publication possible. For their financial support I would like to thank: Audrey and Bernard Bermack, Betsy Brown, Pat Cody, Don Evans, Jeannette Ferrary and Peter Carroll, Herb Freeman, Peter Glazer, Lou and Ann Gordon, Kathryn Hill, Janet (Hannah) Kranzberg, Brian McWilliams, John Penrod, Vivian Raineri, Marci Rubin in honor of Hank Rubin, Rosalie Sennett, Freda Tanz, Nate and Corine Thornton, the Ship Clerk's Association ILWU Local 34, Jack and Joan Shafran, Matt Herron, the Estate of Robert Capa, and Joan and Lucy Balter, the proud and loving daughters of Martin Balter. I would also like to thank Milt Wolff for his twenty-five years of friendship. And I would especially like to acknowledge the editorial and emotional support from my partner, Nancy Van Zwalenburg.

Most importantly, I would like to thank those whose words and pictures appear on these pages, as well as the other veterans of the Abraham Lincoln Brigade, whose lives have been as extraordinary as those mentioned in this book.

FOREWORD PETER N. CARROLL

It would be no exaggeration to say that in 1936, the year the Spanish civil war began, most Americans viewed Spain through a stereotypical lens as a quaint country, the land of bullfights, flamenco dancers, and sun. A popular children's book published that year, *Ferdinand the Bull,* depicted a happy animal that preferred to doze in the shade of a cork tree rather than fight with his horns. So when the Spanish army, led by General Francisco Franco, rebelled against the elected republican government in July 1936, the American public saw little reason for concern.

U.S. economic interests in Spain were modest (though the State Department did worry about what would happen to the Ford and General Motors plants in anarchist Catalonia). Mostly, in this decade of isolationism, foreign conflicts evoked bitter memories of President Woodrow Wilson's futile promises to end all wars in the

last war. Washington officials promptly ordered the citizenry to keep its noses out of Spanish affairs, though the head of Texaco, itching for Franco's revenue, ignored the orders with impunity and sold the fascist rebels U.S. oil on credit. And a trickle of idealistic young men and women, alarmed by German and Italian support for the rebellion and worried about the spread of fascism, quietly began to make their way to Spain to lend what support they could to the embattled government.

In January 1937, the U.S. Congress, concerned about embroiling the nation in another war and with the blessings of President Franklin D. Roosevelt, enacted a neutrality law that prohibited Americans from traveling to Spain. Nevertheless, within a month, some four hundred American volunteers had formed the Abraham Lincoln Battalion to fight the fascists; by the end of

February, they had engaged the enemy at Jarama and suffered their first heavy casualties. Other volunteers continued to enlist, eventually numbering about three thousand (though never that many at any one time). They reinforced the Lincolns, formed two additional battalions—the George Washington and MacKenzie-Papineau (which included Canadians)—and served in various other units, including the John Brown Artillery Battery, the Regiment de Tren (transportation), and the American Medical Bureau. Home front writers called them, collectively, the Abraham Lincoln Brigade.

"Say of them, they were young," wrote the poet Genevieve Taggart; but they weren't *that* young. Their average age was over twenty-eight; one-third were older than thirty-five. Yet fully 80 percent were not married. Although many volunteers were college-educated professionals— doctors, nurses, teachers, journalists, students— the overwhelming majority were ordinary workers. The most frequently listed occupations in the rosters compiled in Spain were seaman, driver, and unemployed. They were, in other words, members of a mobile labor force. In this time of Depression, most did not have rooted careers and could not afford to settle down with families. Interestingly, too, many had grown up in households in which one parent was absent, because of death or divorce. Life in working-class families was not easy in such times.

The Lincolns came from nearly every state in the union, but especially from the nation's cities.

Many were children of European immigrants; records kept in Spain indicate that there were more than fifty European nationality groups represented in the brigade. Estimates suggest that as many as one-third were Jewish. But what especially distinguished their pluralism was the presence of numerous non-whites who were fully integrated in the ranks. Nearly one hundred Lincoln volunteers were African Americans, including battalion commander Oliver Law, perhaps the first black American to command white troops in battle. There were also Native Americans, Asian Americans, Hawaiians, Puerto Ricans, and Filipinos.

This melting pot was no accident, but a deliberate antifascist, antiracist policy of the Communist Party that had created and screened the volunteer army. Approximately 70 percent of the volunteers identified themselves as members of the Communist Party or its affiliate organizations, such as the Young Communist League. In the face of the fascist threat in Europe, the Soviet Union and the Communist International had adopted a new policy, known as the Popular Front, to broaden their base of support among liberal groups. Earl Browder, head of the U.S. Communist Party, said, "communism is twentieth-century Americanism." Such policies made the communist movement attractive to people who were concerned about broad issues of social justice. The Socialist Party also tried to raise a volunteer force to send to Spain, but lacked the international connections to succeed in the face of government opposition. Yet many Socialists found their way into the brigade; some became officers.

The war experience seared the volunteers with a common identity. "We, all of us here," wrote the soldier-poet Edwin Rolfe from Barcelona in 1938, "date a certain birth of ourselves to our arrival here, and since we didn't, most of us, know each other at home, all that we have in common is Spain." Such camaraderie became the stuff of legend, but it was not enough to save the Spanish Republic. Aided by Hitler and Mussolini, Franco's superior forces overwhelmed the international brigades, which were finally withdrawn from battle in 1938. Eight hundred Americans had died in Spain; most of the others had been wounded at least once. For the survivors, Spain was no longer just another country, a geographical place on the map, but a cause, a principle, the reason to continue the struggle against fascism on other fronts.

And Spain has followed the Lincoln veterans for the rest of their lives. As Richard Bermack's *The Front Lines of Social Change* picks up the ensuing story, we see how the Lincoln "vets," as they are known to their friends, dedicated themselves to a variety of political causes. During World War II, they fought a two-front war: first, against U.S. military policy that considered them potential subversives and refused them opportunities to fight overseas; and then, after waging a crusade that won them their rights, they garnered a disproportionate number of battlefield medals for heroism. Meanwhile, at every opportunity, they challenged the army's policies of racial segregation. They also led a public campaign against the Franco dictatorship and helped to persuade the newly formed United Nations to exclude Spain from membership.

As the United States embarked on a Cold War against the Soviet Union, however, the Lincolns became sitting targets in the anticommunist crusade at home. President Harry Truman's attorney general listed the brigade and its veterans' group as subversive organizations; the federal government's Subversive Activities Control Board condemned them as a communist front organization in 1954. For individual veterans, service in Spain became prima facie evidence of subversive activities. Investigated publicly by FBI agents, veterans faced loss of jobs, homes, and normal family life. Several vets went to jail for their political associations. And even when higher courts overturned such miscarriages of justice, vindication usually came years later, after the damage was done.

The Cold War also altered the standing of fascist Spain. Seen, initially, by Presidents Roosevelt and Truman as a pariah nation, Spain emerged in the 1950s as a cornerstone of the anticommunist alliance. During the Eisenhower presidency, Spain signed a formal alliance with the United States and entered the United Nations. While few politicians acknowledged the Lincolns' protests of these policies, the veterans now began to send material assistance to the prisoners of the Franco regime. This aid, which lasted until after Franco's death in 1975, set a precedent for later contributions to other humanitarian causes around the world.

As the political climate changed again during the late 1960s and '70s, the Lincolns discovered growing support from younger generations that shared an antimilitarist outlook. The annual brigade reunions in New York and California began to attract large audiences that honored the men and women who had defied U.S. government policies to aid a democratic country. In the 1980s, the Lincolns won broad public support for their campaign to send ambulances and other medical supplies to embattled countries like Nicaragua and Cuba and to black liberation groups in South Africa. By then, the Lincoln vets stood as elder statesmen of protest movements around the country.

The number of Lincoln survivors continues to dwindle; at this writing in 2004, perhaps fifty or sixty are still alive. None, in my presence, has ever expressed regret about going to Spain. And few have doubted the value of their activist lives since. Indeed, the veterans have taken pains to see that their legacy is preserved, by supporting the Abraham Lincoln Brigade Archives (ALBA), a nonprofit educational organization originally founded by vets twenty-five years ago and dedicated to disseminating the history of America's antifascist movements to younger generations. (See the website www.alba-valb.org.) Some of ALBA's photographs appear in this volume. Paired with Richard Bermack's contemporary portraits, they capture a living history of courage—moral courage—that may inspire all people of conscience.

INTRODUCTION

Staring out into the darkness as the boat made its way across the ocean to Spain in 1936, nurse Hilda Bell Roberts, barely twenty at the time, reflected on her life. "My plans were simple," she recalls. "Get married, have kids, lead an organized life. Then I realized I was giving it all up, and my life would never be the same. It felt good."[1] Roberts is one of three thousand Americans who traveled to Spain in the late 1930s to defend the democratic Republic of Spain against a fascist military takeover. Nearly seventy years later, marching with a crowd of demonstrators protesting U.S. military intervention in Afghanistan and Iraq, she smiles and states with pride, "Going to Spain was the best decision I ever made, next to becoming a nurse."

Since going to Spain, Roberts has participated in the communist movement, the struggle for the eight-hour workday, the civil rights movement, and the Berkeley free speech movement. She opposed the United States war in Vietnam and the production of nuclear weapons. To protest U.S. intervention in Central America, she traveled to Nicaragua with Elders for Survival to harvest coffee. When she was in her seventies, she fasted for twenty-three days to defy the U.S. blockade on Cuba. Every Friday afternoon for over a decade, she has stood in the Women in Black vigil for peace in the Middle East. The Berkeley city council recently celebrated her lifelong commitment to social justice by proclaiming a Hilda Roberts Day. In many ways her life exemplifies those of the veterans of the Abraham Lincoln Brigade.

You won't find their names in most history textbooks. Their goal was to stop the spread of fascism. If the world had followed their lead, World War II might have been prevented.

The 1930s were a time of uncertainty. The fragile democratic republic of Germany crumbled, taken over by Adolph Hitler. Benito Mussolini's Fascist Party took power in Italy and invaded Ethiopia. Then General Francisco

Above: Hilda Roberts's passport, 1936

Opposite: Hilda Roberts demonstrating against the U.S. war in the Middle East, 2002, San Francisco

Franco led a military invasion of Spain, attempting to overthrow the Spanish Republic with a dictatorship of the Falangist Party (Spain's fascist party). And there the line was drawn. *"¡No pasarán!* [They will not pass!] Madrid will be the tomb of fascism," became the rallying cry of people from all over the world. An army of world citizens answered the call of history to defend democracy.

The Spanish civil war lasted from 1936 to 1939. Germany and Italy backed Franco; Czechoslovakia, the Soviet Union, and Mexico supported the Republic. Others remained neutral. This neutrality prevented supplies from being sent to the republican forces, while Italy and Germany successfully sent supplies and military forces to aid Franco, leading to his ultimate victory in 1939. A few months after victorious fascist troops marched down the streets of Madrid, the Nazis marched through Prague, and not long after that, on to Paris.

The Spanish civil war was a journey to hell. One third of the international volunteers were killed. Out of the three thousand Americans who went to Spain, eight hundred gave their lives. Of those who did return, most had been wounded.

During World War II, the United States government labeled the Spanish civil war volunteers "premature antifascists." After World War II, many were blacklisted, hounded by the FBI, and jailed. But they did not give up. The Veterans of the Abraham Lincoln Brigade continued to fight for those oppressed and exploited by the powerful. They fought for social justice and equality: the right of all human beings to food, clothing, shelter, education, and health care, and to be free from religious and ethnic intolerance and the ravages of war.

This "good fight" would give meaning and a sense of purpose to the rest of their lives. Even when the organization many of them identified with, the Communist Party of the United States, proved to be a failed god, their individual moral compasses led them to keep on marching.

What core beliefs gave these men and women such a rich sense of purpose throughout their lives, even when the world turned against them? Milt Wolff, the last commander of the Abraham Lincoln Battalion and later the commander of the Veterans of the Abraham Lincoln Brigade, states, "The only thing that gives any purpose to life is to move humankind along to a better world, the struggle to eliminate homelessness, hunger, disease, and most of all, to eliminate the greatest insanity, war. That is the 'good fight.'" Ruth Davidow, a nurse in the Spanish civil war, states, "I can't live in the world if I can't fight against injustice."[2] As seaman Bill Bailey, another veteran, would say, they were "stand-up guys," people who would fight for the rights of others.

Every year, legislators, Pulitzer prize–winning authors, other dignitaries, and a multitude of friends, family, and admirers meet in New York and in the San Francisco Bay Area to honor these dedicated volunteers who never gave up. In the

"The only thing that gives any purpose to life is to move humankind along to a better world, the struggle to eliminate homelessness, hunger, disease, and most of all, to eliminate the greatest insanity, war. That is the 'good fight.'"

Author photo for Milt Wolff's autobiographical novel, *Another Hill*, Berkeley, California, 1993

1980s, I began photographing the vets at their reunions and at other events, and in 1999 I began working on their publication, *The Volunteer*. I was seduced by both their dedication and their cantankerousness. At a time when social movements were falling apart and cynicism and greed were overtaking humanism, here was a group of very colorful individuals who had been able to keep a sense of community for over half a century, even when doing so put them at odds with society as a whole. In this book I have combined my photos of the vets with photos from the Abraham Lincoln Brigade Archives and from the vets' personal files, along with interviews and other material, to tell their story.

Notes:

1. All quotations in this book, unless otherwise noted, are from interviews and other personal communication with the author.
2. Judy Montell, *Forever Activists: Stories from the Abraham Lincoln Brigade,* documentary film, 1990

Above: Coleman Persily and Angela Davis at the 2002 VALB reunion, Oakland, California, 2002

Opposite: Ed Bender (left) and Bill Sennett, Oakland, 1993

PRELUDE TO WAR

The Spanish civil war followed a turning point in history: the abdication of Alfonso XIII in 1931 and the establishment of the Spanish Republic had signaled the end of feudalism in Europe. Spain had been ruled by a monarchy and the Catholic Church since the final conquest of the Moors in 1492. Religion was used ideologically to control the population, and when that failed, the military brutally suppressed any opposition. Religions other than Catholicism were outlawed; heretics were tortured by the Inquisition and burnt at the stake, a practice that continued in Spain through the mid-nineteenth century. Until the Republic was established, the Spanish ruling class was among the wealthiest of Europe, while the largely illiterate Spanish peasants were among the poorest. All welfare services, education, and health care were controlled by the church. Those out of favor with the church literally starved to death.

The brutal conditions of the Spanish peasants are described by Constancia de la Mora in her autobiography, *In Place of Splendor.*[1] Mora grew up in one of the richest families in Spain. Her grandfather was prime minister, but Constancia, moved by the poverty of the people her grandfather ruled, became a social worker. In her autobiography she describes villages where people were so poor and undernourished that their growth and mental abilities were stunted; their average height was only about four feet. A loaf of bread was a luxury for the villagers, while the local church officials lived well.

The Republic changed all that, initiating universal education, land reform, health care, nutrition programs, and social services for all. The new constitution, similar to the United States Constitution, ended religious intolerance and gave new rights to women. For the first time, divorce became legal in Spain.

The Spanish Republic initiated reforms and social services to ameliorate the brutal poverty of the Spanish peasants. Photo by Sam Walters

Right: An orphanage of the Spanish Republic. *Peoples Weekly World*/Reference Center for Marxist Studies

Below: Spanish civilians at a barricade defending Madrid. In response to the military invasion by Franco, the Republic opened its armories and armed the Spanish people, who stopped the initial invasion. At that point Hitler and Mussolini sent troops to aid Franco. *Peoples Weekly World*/Reference Center for Marxist Studies

The triumph of enlightenment and democracy in Europe did not last for long. In 1933 Adolph Hitler and the National Socialist German Workers' (Nazi) Party came to power in Germany, replacing the German republic with one of the most brutal dictatorships in human history. Benito Mussolini and the Fascist Party took over Italy.

When, in 1936, Spanish General Francisco Franco and the Falangists invaded Spain from Morocco and led a military uprising against the Republic, the government of the Republic armed the workers and peasants who, along with troops loyal to the Republic, defeated the uprising at Madrid and Barcelona. It would have ended there, but Hitler and Mussolini came to the aid of the Spanish fascists, sending planes and fifty thousand troops to aid Franco. The German air force bombed the ancient city of Guérnica. The use of technology against a civilian population heralded the beginning of modern warfare. The atrocities became the subject of *Guérnica,* one of Pablo Picasso's most famous paintings. The same German Luftwaffe that got its training bombing Spanish cities would later bomb London.

Notes
1. Constancia de la Mora, *In Place of Splendor: The Autobiography of a Spanish Woman* (New York: Harcourt, Brace and Co., 1939)

THE GREAT DEPRESSION

Many Americans could easily identify with the suffering of the Spanish people. The United States was, with much of the world, in the midst of the Great Depression. One-fourth of all Americans were out of work. The stock market crash of 1929 had led to massive bank failures. Nine thousand banks closed, taking with them the life savings of their depositors. Poor people became even more impoverished, and many families who had made a good living during the 1920s suddenly had nothing to eat and nowhere to live. In 1932, at least twenty-five thousand families and more than two hundred thousand young people wandered the nation seeking food, clothing, shelter, and jobs. Many cities were filling up with tent encampments, and Dust Bowl refugees traveled across the country. For many, the popular song "Brother Can You Spare a Dime" characterized the era.[1]

Mass rally at Madison Square Garden supporting the Spanish Republic, 1936. *Peoples Weekly World*/Reference Center for Marxist Studies

Above: Nate Thornton (left) in Spain.
Thornton personal collection

Right: Nate Thornton, Oakland, 2000

Nate Thornton's father lost his job in 1929, right after the market crash. From then on, it was one job after another, never quite being able to make ends meet. The family had traveled from Utah to Fresno to San Francisco looking for work. Finally Nate's father was reduced to begging county agencies for relief. The family was walking down the street after leaving one agency when a man handed them a flyer inviting them to attend a meeting. "We liked what they had to say," Thornton recalls:

They explained that the man who owns the factory pays someone forty dollars to produce eighty dollars' worth of goods, which then sit in a warehouse until he sells them. If he has too many goods stocked up to sell, then he lays people off. Why should people starve in a country with all this wealth because the capitalists have warehouses full of goods and won't share their profits with those who made it for them?

Nate joined the Young Communist League (YCL), and his father joined the Communist Party. The two of them would later travel together to Spain to defend the Republic.

In 1929 the wealthiest 0.1 percent of Americans had a combined income equal to the bottom 42 percent and controlled 34 percent of all savings; 80 percent of Americans had no savings at all. At a time when the average annual personal income was $750, Henry Ford reported a personal income of $14 million.[2] This disparity was seen as one of the causes of the Depression and led to widespread social unrest. Similar conditions existed throughout the world, and a growing labor movement rose up to challenge the inequality worldwide. Despotic leaders seized on the desperation of the poor, exploiting racism, religious intolerance, and fear of immigrants, blaming the economic problems and the misery people were suffering on scapegoats. Fascist dictators took power in Germany, Italy, and Portugal, and fascist parties grew in England and France. In the United States, popular radio orators like Father Coughlin praised Hitler and Mussolini.

The other response was a call for more equal distribution of wealth, based on equality for all races, occupations, and ethnic groups. The labor movement gained strength with mottos such as "An injury to one is an injury to all." People joined Unemployed Councils to help those without jobs get relief. Thornton describes their activities:

We would picket offices to get people on relief, until they could get a regular payment for food and rent. One time we heard that someone was about to be evicted. We got there and their belongings were out on the street, so we moved them back in their apartment. Then the police came and moved them back out, so we took their things down to Civic Center and set up a tent. We talked to anyone who came by, and they would stop and listen. Finally the police took up a collection among themselves to put the people back in their house.

In the YCL, Thornton listened to firebrand Archie Brown. Brown talked about Spain and how the Spanish people were going to create a socialist society in which the workers would run the factories to produce food and clothing for everyone, instead of for the profit of a few. "We couldn't make a living here, and we thought Spain would be a good country to live in after the war," says Thornton.[3]

On the other side of the country, over one hundred thousand people rallied in New York City's Union Square to protest the effects of unemployment. Teenager Saul Wellman cut school to attend the demonstration, which turned into a riot. Wellman was expelled from school, along with all the other kids the authorities believed had attended the demonstration.

Wellman's mother was active in organizing the needle trades. "I grew up sucking socialism from my mother's breast," he brags. Wellman describes the spirit of the times:

A socialist [Norman Thomas] ran for president of the United States and got almost a million votes. Five socialists were members of the New York state legislature, and two were congressmen. At the same time, there was a violent anti-labor and anti-black attitude, but you could sense there was an opening for change.[4]

Wellman joined the YCL and became a soap-box orator at sixteen, standing on street corners and delivering speeches denouncing social injustice. He became a delivery truck driver at seventeen and then organized his fellow drivers into a union. The next year he became a full-time union organizer and began his lifelong career as a self-described professional revolutionary. It seemed only natural for him to go to Spain along with other YCL members from his neighborhood, including Abe Smorodin, Lou Gordon, and Maury Colow.

Milt Wolff's father was a successful entrepreneur until the Depression hit. The family was forced to move to Coney Island, where they could barely make ends meet. Wolff had to drop out of high school and join the Civilian Conservation Corps, a government jobs program focusing on public works that housed and fed workers in camps throughout the nation. There he got his first taste of collective action. In response to the poor quality of food in their camp, Wolff's roommate organized a strike. When the strike succeeded, Wolff was bitten by the bug of political struggle. He became a member of the YCL.

The young Wolff excelled as an orator. In fact, at one meeting he delivered a speech so moving, calling for volunteers to go to Spain, that without thinking he volunteered himself. "I told my parents I was going to Spain because I got a job working in a factory. Later my cover was blown

Above: Saul Wellman in Spain. Tamiment Library, Abraham Lincoln Brigade Archives, New York University

Left: Saul Wellman, Oakland, 1986

Above: Abe Smorodin (left) and Lou Gordon, just before leaving for Spain, c. 1936. Gordon personal collection

Right: Abe Smorodin (left) and Lou Gordon in New York, 2001

when I appeared in a photograph on the front page of the *Forward* (the Jewish newspaper) with Hemingway."

For most of the volunteers, the Communist Party provided the resources and organizational vehicle for getting to Spain. Many of the vets had been members of the Young Communist League or were actively involved in the party itself. Others, like Dave Smith, did not consider their motivation to be political. They were drawn to the fight for justice by moral beliefs and their reaction to the economic injustices around them.

Those who went to Spain have been characterized as coming from immigrant Jewish socialist and communist backgrounds. That was true for many, but it was not universally so. Perley Payne, a vet and a descendant of pioneers,

grew up in a small town where streets were named after his ancestors. "Spain was the first time I met Jewish people and nonwhites," he states.

Applied physics professor Ted Veltfort was raised an Episcopalian and became politicized in a Baptist boarding school run by progressives. In college he helped organize the American Student Union:

We started as a liberal organization debating about capitalism and socialism and racism. It soon became clear that we needed an economy that was run for the benefit of the public and not the corporations. We went from anticapitalist to socialist to communist, because the communists were the most effective. I didn't think twice about going to Spain.

Notes
1. Robert S. McElvaine, *The Great Depression: America, 1929–1941* (New York: Times Books, 1984)
2. Ibid.
3. Thornton is the only vet that I know of who mentioned the possibility of living in Spain after the war as a reason for going.
4. Judy Montell, interview with Saul Wellman, 1998

Top: Perley Payne in San Francisco, 1992

Bottom: Milt Wolff and Ernest Hemingway. Photograph by Robert Capa, from The Bancroft Library, University of California

THE SPANISH CIVIL WAR

The Spanish Republic had been formed by a coalition ranging politically from right to left, including everything in between; and economically from members of the Spanish middle-class intelligentsia who wanted to bring their nation into the twentieth century to peasants and workers who wanted to escape from poverty. Opposing the Republic were the church and the old aristocracy.

The Catholic Church responded to its loss of power in Spain by organizing international opposition to the Spanish Republic. Pope Pius XI blessed Franco's "crusade" and denounced the Republic's "truly satanic hatred of God."[1] After centuries of persecution by the church, many of the peasants took revenge, committing atrocities against priests and nuns, fueling the church's accusations that the republican loyalists were godless communists.

The forty thousand volunteers who traveled to Spain from all over the world to defend the Republic formed a rather curious army. Throughout history, mercenaries have fought in countries other than their own, but they have usually been professional soldiers. The international volunteers were artists, intellectuals, and workers who felt a moral imperative to put down their paintbrushes, pens, and tools and pick up guns. "Most of us were pacifists. We were fighting to stop war," Milt Wolff states. *Saturday Night Fever* producer Milt Felsen, a vet who later went to work for the Directors Guild of America, echoed these sentiments in his autobiography, *The Anti-Warrior*.[2] In later life the vets would become prominent scientists, doctors, lawyers, business people, writers, movie producers, visual artists, and social workers.

Once the volunteers arrived in Spain, any romantic notions they might have had about

"Every action you went into, you were scared."

Above: Dave Smith (right, holding banner) after the battle of Jarama. Smith private collection

Left: Dave Smith, 1996

Above: Marion Wachtel Merriman and Robert Merriman. Robert Merriman was one of the first commanders of the Lincoln Brigade and was killed in Spain. Marion was one of the few women in combat in the Lincoln Brigade. She later became the commander of the Bay Area VALB Post. The Bancroft Library, University of California

Right: Marion Wachtel Merriman, Oakland, 1985

war quickly evaporated. The first contingent of Americans to arrive were nearly all killed or wounded in their first battle, the battle for Jarama Valley. The commander of the 15th International Brigade, Vladimir Copic, ordered Robert Merriman to undertake this defense of the Madrid-Valencia road in order to keep the fascist forces from cutting off Madrid. The volunteers were armed with WWI-vintage rifles and machine guns that barely worked. Merriman informed Copic that without the artillery and armored support the brigade had been promised, the assault would be futile and suicidal. Copic threatened Merriman with court martial if he didn't attack. The ensuing battle resembled Tennyson's "Charge of the Light Brigade": the promised support failed to materialize, and the valley became a graveyard for the advancing troops.

The war attracted many sympathetic journalists, such as photographer Robert Capa and writers Ernest Hemingway, Martha Gellhorn, and Herbert L. Matthews. After interviewing survivors of Jarama, Hemingway labeled the attack "idiotic," an example of "monumental stupidity." Jarama became known as the volunteers' baptism by fire.

The volunteers were heroic in carrying out orders and standing up under fire. As Peter N. Carroll writes in his definitive *Odyssey of the Abraham Lincoln Brigade*,[3] "The Lincolns acquired a reputation for courage and valor, the heroism of shock troops, that became part of their mythology."

The names of the battlefields, like Hill 666, Gandesa, Teruel (nicknamed "the North Pole"), the Aragon front, and Ebro, still bring a chill to many of the vets. Fifty years later, returning to Spain for a veterans' reunion, Mel Anderson was overcome by fear as he took his son on a tour of the wheat fields of Brunete, where one of the fiercest battles took place. Two American battalions went into the battle, but only enough for one battalion survived.

One of the unique elements of the Spanish civil war was the presence of commissars: in addition to military commanders, there were Communist Party functionaries whose duty was political indoctrination. Some of the commissars, like labor organizer Steve Nelson, were well received. They continued the troops' education about why they were fighting, kept a moral focus, and strengthened their commitment to the struggle. However, many of the commissars were seen as privileged middle-class ideologues and were resented by the rank and file. Abe Osheroff, himself a rank-and-file Young Communist League organizer, remembers a song they used to sing to announce a commissar's arrival: "Hurray for Barnum and Bailey," it began, "The circus is coming to town," and ended with a line about watching out for elephant shit.

Jarama
(to the tune of "Red River Valley")

There's a valley in Spain called Jarama.
It's a place that we all know so well.
It was there that we gave of our
    manhood,
Where so many of our brave
    comrades fell.
We are proud of the Lincoln Battalion
And the fight for Madrid that it made.
There we fought like true sons of
    the people
As part of the Fifteenth Brigade.
Now we're far from that valley of
    sorrow,
But its memory we ne'er will forget.
So before we conclude this reunion
Let us stand to our glorious dead.

—Song of the Abraham Lincoln Brigade

Above: Mel Anderson (left) with his machine gun company. Fifty years later he shook with fear remembering the battle of Brunete. The Bancroft Library, University of California

Right: Mel Anderson, Oakland, 1986

Above: Dr. John Simon in Spain. Tamiment Library, Abraham Lincoln Brigade Archives, New York University

Left: Hy Tabb (left) and Dr. John Simon, New York, 1997

Above: Bill Wheeler in Spain. Tamiment
Library, Abraham Lincoln Brigade Archives,
New York University

Right: Bill Wheeler in Oakland, 1986

Above: Matti Mattson (left) next to a bulletin board in Spain. Tamiment Library, Abraham Lincoln Brigade Archives, New York University

Left: Matti Mattson, New York, 1999

Above: (Left to right) Don Thayer, Manny Lanser, Milt Wolff, George Watt, Harold Smith, and Archie Brown. Hon Brown personal collection

Right: Manny Lanser, New York, 1997

Above: Morris Brier in Spain. Tamiment Library, Abraham Lincoln Brigade Archives, New York University, Fifteenth International Brigade Photographic Unit Photograph Collection

Left: Morris Brier, 1988

Above: Mark Billings in Spain. Billings personal collection

Right: Mark Billings at the 1997 VALB reunion in Oakland

Above: Bob Reed in Spain. Reed personal collection

Left: Bob Reed, Seattle, 1993

Above: Norman Berkowitz behind a machine gun next to
Jack Shafran at Albalate del Arzobiso, September 1937.
Berkowitz personal collection

Right: Norman (Normie) Berkowitz, New York, 1999

Above: Jack Freeman (holding the brigade mascot) and Ernest Amatniek. Freeman was killed in Spain. Herb Freeman personal collection

Left: Ernest Amatniek, New York, 1997

Above: Harry Fisher, c. 1936. Harry Fisher personal collection

Right: Harry Fisher, New York, 1997. Fisher became well known in the 1990s as an anti-war activist. He died in New York in 2003, in his nineties, of a heart attack at one of the large demonstrations against the U.S. war in Iraq. He authored the book *Comrades, Tales of a Brigadista in the Spanish Civil War.*

Above: Carl Geiser in Spain. Geiser was a commissar of the MacPaps, Canadian volunteers. He was captured eight days after this photo was taken and spent the rest of the war in prison. Geiser personal collection

Left: Carl Geiser, Oakland, 1995

Hello
my name is

Above: Sam Schiff in Spain. Alan Rom personal collection

Right: Sam Schiff, New York, 1997

Above: Herman (Gabby) Rosenstein in Spain.
Tamiment Library, Abraham Lincoln Brigade
Archives, New York University

Left: Gabby Rosenstein, Oakland, 1982

Above: Harry Randall, one of the 15th Brigade's photographers, c. 1936. He took many of the archival photos in this book. Tamiment Library, Abraham Lincoln Brigade Archives, New York University

Right: Harry Randall in New York, 2003

Above: Bill Susman (left) conferring with Joe Brandy and John Gerlack in a dugout trench in Spain, 1937. Tamiment Library, Abraham Lincoln Brigade Archives, New York University, Fifteenth International Brigade Photographic Unit Photograph Collection

Left: Bill Susman, New York, 1997

Above: Toby Jensky in Spain

Right: Toby Jensky, Oakland, 1986

Opposite page: American nurses, 1938. Left to right: Rose Weiner, Norah Temple, Toby Jensky, Anna Taft, Sana Goldblatt, and Selma Chadwick, with Spanish nurse's aides Andrea and Leoncia. Tamiment Library, Abraham Lincoln Brigade Archives, New York University, Fifteenth International Brigade Photographic Unit Photograph Collection

Medical Conditions

Medical conditions were primitive. "I saw a lot of people with terrible wounds and destruction," states Hilda Roberts. Lacking proper medical equipment, medical personnel had to clean the wounds as best they could. Roberts recalls having to perform tracheotomies on solders without the use of tubes or modern antibiotics. Roberts cared for the wounded at the battle of Teruel and then during the last offensive by the Abraham Lincoln Battalion and their retreat across the Ebro River. "I was with Dr. Friedman and a couple of nurses.

We got all of our patients out except one who was beyond help. He didn't make it across before they blew up the bridge to slow down the fascists." With the bridge blown up, many soldiers were forced to swim across the river against the raging current. Many didn't make it. Ernest Hemingway was so moved that he went down to the water to greet the swimmers as they staggered out of the river. Roberts remembers him visiting the wounded in the makeshift hospital. When she saw him a year later in New York, he remarked that he had just finished writing a book about the war, *For Whom the Bell Tolls*.[4]

The Medical Brigade

No Americans contributed more to the struggle against fascism than those who put their life-saving skills to work for the Spanish people and the international volunteers. Yet to this day, their magnificent record is relatively unknown. They are the least mentioned of all our heroes....They, too, were poorly equipped for their terrible workload. Everything needed—medicine, bandages, needles, anesthesia, x-ray equipment, etc.—was in short supply. Nevertheless, they worked day and night, often under fire, in first-aid stations, field and base hospitals, giving aid and comfort, saving limbs and lives of Spaniards and Internationals.

In addition, they made outstanding advances in the field of military medicine. Triage, mobile surgical units, and whole blood transfusion made their first appearances under the leadership of Dr. Edward Barsky, Dr. Jolly, and Dr. Norman Bethune [Canadian].

Many of us would have been disabled and many less of us alive today were it not for the work of the American Medical Service.

—From *No Pasaran! The 50th Anniversary of the Abraham Lincoln Brigade*, published by the Abraham Lincoln Brigade Archives

Above: Hank Rubin in his clinical laboratory at the base hospital in Spain, 1937. Rubin personal collection

Right: Hank Rubin, Oakland, 1986

Far left: Mildred Rackley Simon, Oakland, 1986

Left: Hospital administrator Mildred Rackley Simon pointing out a bullet hole in an ambulance in Spain. Tamiment Library, Abraham Lincoln Brigade Archives, New York University

Below: Ruth Davidow (second from right) and ambulance driver Evelyn Hutchins returned from Spain during the war to tour college campuses in the United States and raise money to support the Lincoln Brigade and send ambulances to Spain. *Peoples Weekly World*/Reference Center for Marxist Studies

The Spanish People

What was it that enabled the veterans to keep up their courage and beliefs in spite of every type of adversity, including disorganized leadership and lack of food, medical supplies, and clothing? For many it was the Spanish people who made it clear what the struggle was all about. Dave Smith, who fought with the Tom Mooney machine gun company, says:[5]

Spain changed my whole life. I saw a country struggling—ordinary people, peasants, poor people. They couldn't even read or write, but when these young people came up to the front, we became an integrated army, the people struggling against the oppressing group of fascists. It left an indelible impression on my mind. So when I got back, I decided that I was going to be committed to furthering the cause of the people, whatever I did.

Dave's arm was badly injured in Spain, but the sacrifice was worth it to him. "Spain was the most important thing I did in my life next to getting married. I didn't feel bitter about the arm." Hilda Roberts was equally moved:

They were wonderful, hard-working people. Most of them were so poor they never had medical care before. They didn't know what a doctor was. If you were not rich, you never saw a doctor or a nurse. I treated one girl with a shrapnel wound, and she was so thankful. She never dreamed that

A school of the Spanish Republic. *Peoples Weekly World*/Reference Center for Marxist Studies

she would be cared for by a nurse or be treated in a hospital.

The majority of the Spanish people Roberts met were illiterate, but they understood what democracy and equality meant, and they were willing to die for it:

There was this one poster that said, "¿Qué haces tu para la victoria?" [What are you doing for victory?] And I remember this one peasant girl. She would point to the poster and say, "I scrub floors." Whatever they did, they felt it was for freedom and democracy.

Above: Sam Walters used to have dinner with this Spanish family during the war. Walters personal collection

Left: Sam Walters, New York, 1997. Walters was an unofficial brigade photographer.

International "Neutrality"

Although many expected the other democratic nations to come to the aid of the Spanish Republic, this did not happen. Europe was still recovering from the trauma and devastation of World War I, and the Italian invasion of Ethiopia in 1935 had nearly brought on another war. The French socialist government of Leon Blum initially agreed to support the Spanish Republic, but French conservatives and the British pressured Blum to close the French border and avoid conflict with Germany. France and England organized a non-intervention committee aimed at preventing the war in Spain from escalating. Twenty-eight countries signed the committee's non-intervention agreement, which prohibited the member nations' citizens from participating in the Spanish civil war. Germany and Italy signed the agreement but continued to aid Franco.

Len Levenson with a group of New York University students in Spain. Tamiment Library, Abraham Lincoln Brigade Archives, New York University, Fifteenth International Brigade Photographic Unit Photograph Collection

The only major power to aid the Spanish Republic was the Soviet Union. Hitler had linked communism and Judaism as the enemies of Germany. Fascism was therefore perceived as a direct threat to the Soviet Union. The USSR organized international brigades, and forty thousand people from fifty-three countries, many defying their governments, traveled to Spain to defend the Republic by joining the brigades or the medical services.[6] The civil war was soon seen as a war between communism and fascism ideologically, and between Germany and the Soviet Union politically. The British, and to a lesser degree the French, were quite willing to let the two sides fight it out, hoping they would devour each other.

In the United States, the Catholic Church pressured President Roosevelt to continue the United States's isolationist policy toward Europe. The Neutrality Act was passed, making it illegal for U.S. citizens to fight in Spain. Passports were stamped "not valid for travel to Spain." To get their passports, the volunteers gave all kinds of spurious reasons for their trips to Europe. Bill Bailey claimed to be an archeologist; Milt Wolff claimed to be searching for a long-lost relative.

With the border between Spain and France sealed off, volunteers en route to Spain were forced to travel a hazardous route over the Pyrenees. The route by sea was even more dangerous, as German and Italian submarines were patrolling the Spanish coast. The boat Abe Osheroff was on sunk, and he was forced to

Passport Not Valid for Travel in Spain

The other day a friend of mine—a kindly old gentleman with pince-nez glasses and a long gray beard—applied for a passport. He was going to Holland and Switzerland to study cheese.

"You are not going to Spain, are you?" asked the man at the desk.

"Heavens, no," said the old gentleman. I am going to Switzerland to study cheese. Why do you ask?"

"Oh, nothing, nothing," said the clerk. "I was just wondering."

After due formalities, the old man received his passport. Adjusting his glasses and opening it at random, he observed a paragraph rubber-stamped in red ink: "This passport is not valid for travel to or in any foreign state in connection with entrance into or service in foreign military or naval forces."

And as if that were not enough, directly under it: "This passport is not valid for travel in Spain." And to make it completely emphatic: "*Este pasaporte no es válido para viajar en España.*" And finally: "*Ce passeport n'est pas valable pour voyager en Espagne.*"

"Good gracious sakes," said the old gentleman, "what is happening to the world?"

"These are troubling times," sighed the clerk."I don't know what to think. No one who comes in here is going to Spain. Some of them are going to Paris to study art, some of them intend to photograph the cathedrals, some of them want to see the Sphinx—I even had one man who said he was going abroad to study spots on the moon." The clerk sighed. "But somehow, they all seem to end up in Spain in the loyalist trenches."

"It's incredible," said the old gentleman.

"And you," said the clerk, "are you going to Switzerland to study cheese? What am I to think?"

"Ah well," said the old man. "Ah well." He turned the passport upside down and a pink slip fell out. Unfolding it carefully, he read: "You will note that the enclosed passport is endorsed 'Not valid for travel in Spain.' Accordingly, the use of the passport for that purpose without obtaining an appropriate amendment thereto by the Department or by an American consular or diplomatic officer will constitute a violation of Section 221 of Title 22 of the United States Code, which makes it unlawful to use a passport in violation of the conditions or restrictions contained therein."

"All this," said the old gentleman, "suggests to me that the tide of traffic toward Spain must be exceedingly great."

"It is the policy of America," said the clerk, "to encourage its citizens to take a neutral attitude toward foreign conflicts."

"Do you mean that the person should be indifferent to which side wins or loses?"

"That seems to be the idea," said the clerk.

"For a man to be indifferent about a vital issue the outcome of which will affect the whole world and everyone living, he would, of course," said the old gentleman, "have to be an absolute ass."

"Yes," said the clerk, "I believe that would be necessary."

—Mike Quin
(first published in the *People's World*)

Archie Brown's passport photos, taken in preparation for the trip to Spain. Hon Brown personal collection

Abe Osheroff (right) with Martín Espada after Espada read this poem at the
New York VALB reunion, 1999

The Carpenter Swam to Spain
For Abe Osheroff and the veterans of the Abraham Lincoln Brigade
by Martín Espada

The ship hushed the waves to sleep at midnight:
Ciudad de Barcelona, Ciudad de Barcelona.
In the name of the aristocrat strolling through his garden
Franco's tanks crawled like a plague of smoldering beetles;
in the name of the bishop and his cathedrals
the firing squads sang a stuttering mass with smoke in their throats;
in the name of the exiled king and blueshirts on the march
bombers with swastika fins sowed an inferno
in village marketplaces and the ribs of the dead.
At Guernica an ancient woman in black stumbled
across a corpse and clawed her hair;
at Víznar, where the spring bubbles, a poet in white shoes
coughed the bullets' blood onto his white shirt,
gypsy sobbing in the cave of his mouth.

Ciudad de Barcelona: The ship plowed the ocean,
and the ocean was a wheat field thinking of bread.
And the faces at the portholes thinking: Spain.

In España, the carpenters and miners kneeled with rifles
behind a barricade of killed horses,
the peasant boys cradled grenades like pomegranates
to fling against the plague of tanks, the hive of helmets.
Elsewhere across the earth, thousands more laid hammers
in toolboxes, holstered drills, promised letters home,
and crowded onto ships for Spain:
volunteers for the Republic, congregation of berets,
fedoras and fist-salutes for the camera, cigarettes and union songs.
The handle of the hammer became the stock of the rifle.

The ship called *Ciudad de Barcelona* steamed
across the thumping tide, hull bearded with foam,
the body of Spain slumbering on the horizon.

Another carpenter read the newspapers by the tunnel-light
of the subway in Brooklyn.
Abe Osheroff sailed for Spain. Because Franco's mustache
was stiff as a paintbrush with his cousins' blood:
because Hitler's iron maw would be a bulldozer,
heaving a downpour of cadavers into common graves.

The ship of volunteers was *Ciudad de Barcelona*,
Abe the carpenter among them, and for them
the word *Barcelona* tingled like the aftertaste of a kiss.
Two miles from shore, they saw the prop plane hover
as if a spectre from the last war,
the pilot's hand jab untranslated warning.
Then the thud, a heart kicking in spasm,
the breastbone of the ship punctured
by a torpedo from Mussolini's submarine.
In seven minutes, the ship called *Ciudad de Barcelona*
tilted and slid into the gushing sea,
at every porthole a face trapped,
mouth round and silent like the porthole.

Eighty mouths round in the high note of silence.
Schultz, captain of the Brooklyn College swim team,
pinned below deck and drowned,
his champion's breaststroke flailing.
Other hands that could swim burst through the wave-walls
and reached for the hands that could not. The boats

of a fishing village crystallized from the foam,
a fleet of saints with salt glistening in their beards,
blankets and rum on the shore.

Abe swam two miles to Spain,
made trowels of his hands
to cleave the thickening water.
His fingers learned the rifle's trigger
as they knew the hammer's claw.
At Fuentes de Ebro, Armageddon
babbled and wailed above the trenches;
when he bled there, an ocean of shipwreck
surged through his body. Today, his white beard
is a garland of clouds and sea-foam,
and he remembers Schultz, the swimmer.

Now, for Abe, I tap these words
like a telegraph operator
with news of survivors:
Ciudad de Barcelona, Ciudad de Barcelona.

Reprinted from *The Volunteer* (1998)

Above (left to right): Seattle vets Jack Koble, Brook Carmichael, and Bob Ingalls. The Bancroft Library, University of California

Right: Brook Carmichael, Seattle, 1998

Bob Ingalls, Seattle, 1998

Needless to catalogue heroes. No man
weighted with rifle, digging with nails in earth,
quickens at the name. Hero's a word for
peacetime. Battle
knows only three realities: enemy, rifle, life.

No man knows war or its meaning who has not
stumbled from tree to tree, desperate for cover,
or dug his face deep in earth, felt the ground pulse
   with
the ear-breaking fall of death. No man knows war
who never has crouched in his foxhole, hearing
the bullets an inch from his head, nor the zoom of
planes like a Ferris wheel strafing the trenches…

War is your comrade struck dead beside you,
his shared cigarette still alive in your lips.

from "City of Anguish" by Edwin Rolfe,
poet laureate of the Abraham Lincoln Brigade

swim to shore. Others were temporarily detained by the French police. There are many tales of heroism during the journey, before the volunteers even got to Spain.

Before long, the concept of "international neutrality" moved from lack of support to outright embargo. The USSR had resources to offer but had no easy way to get supplies to Spain. Occasionally France would open its borders for a short period, but by and large, supplies for the Republic piled up on the French side, unable to get through, effectively starving the loyalists. Meanwhile, Italy and Germany had no trouble supplying Franco's forces. While, in the name of neutrality, the United States attempted to prevent its citizens from aiding the Republic, industrialists like Ford and corporations like Texaco aided Franco by giving him oil and petroleum on credit.

Dave Smith describes the volunteers' frustration:

Every action you went into, you were scared. I knew after the second action that unless we got more equipment it was a losing cause. We had rifles and were going up against submachine guns and artillery. We felt betrayed that they wouldn't open up the borders to allow our supplies to get through. We were so angry at the so-called democratic countries that we were determined to fight like hell up until the end. I was angry—here was this battle to save this country, and three thousand guys could see what was happening, and

the rest of the world knew, and they were willing to appease Hitler. As long as he didn't attack them, they didn't care.

Without sufficient ammunition, food, or water, the republican forces were unable to fight effectively against the well-supplied opposition troops. Nevertheless, the volunteers kept fighting. "Men who were sent home wounded came back to fight again. During the big battles, the hospitals would empty. Every American volunteer would leave the hospital to fight," states Milt Wolff.

"After that terrible defeat at Teruel, when we lost half of our forces, we mobilized, trained, and launched the last great offensive of the war, the Ebro offensive," Wolff recalls. In July of 1938, the republican troops crossed the Ebro River and routed Franco's forces. But without supplies and ammunition, they were forced to retreat.

In September of 1938, British Prime Minister Neville Chamberlain signed the Munich Pact with Hitler, agreeing that Germany could annex part of Czechoslovakia. The pact, which Chamberlain hailed as securing "peace in our time," banished any hope of the European powers taking a stand against Hitler or stopping the fascists from overrunning Spain. Realizing the end was near, the republican government decided to send the international forces home. Many of them would have been willing to fight to their deaths—especially those from Italy and Germany, who had nowhere to return to.

Farewell Speech to the International Brigades

by Dolores Ibarruri, "La Pasionaria" (edited version)
Barcelona, October 1938

It is hard to say a few words in farewell to the heroes of the international brigades, both because of what they are and what they represent.

A feeling of sorrow, an infinite grief catches our throats...sorrow for those who are going away, for the soldiers of the highest ideal of human redemption, exiles from their countries, persecuted by the tyrants of all peoples...grief for those who will stay here forever, mingling with the Spanish soil or in the very depths of our hearts, bathed in the light of our gratitude.

You came to us from all peoples, from all races. You came like brothers of ours, like sons of undying Spain; and in the hardest days of the war, when the capital of the Spanish republic was threatened, it was you, gallant comrades of the international brigades, who helped to save the city with your fighting enthusiasm, your heroism, and your spirit of sacrifice.

For the first time in the history of the peoples' struggles, there has been the spectacle, breathtaking in its grandeur, of the formation of international brigades to help save a threatened country's freedom and independence, the freedom and independence of our Spanish land.

They gave us everything: their youth and their maturity; their science or their experience; their blood and their lives: their hopes and aspirations; and they asked us for nothing at all. That is to say, they did want a post in the struggle, they did aspire to the honor of dying for us.

Mothers! Women! When the years pass by and the wounds of the war are being staunched; when the cloudy memory of the sorrowful, bloody days returns in a present of freedom, peace, and well-being; when the feelings of rancor are dying away and when pride in a free country is felt equally by all Spaniards, then speak to your children. Tell them of these men of the international brigades.

Tell them how, coming over seas and mountains, crossing frontiers bristling with bayonets, watched for by raving dogs thirsting to tear at their flesh, these men reached our country as crusaders for freedom, to fight and die for Spain's liberty and independence, which were threatened by German and Italian fascism.

Today they are going away. Many of them, thousands of them, are staying here with the Spanish earth for their shroud, and all Spaniards remember them with the deepest feeling.

Comrades of the international brigades: political reasons, reasons of state, the welfare of that same cause for which you offered your blood with boundless generosity, are sending you back, some of you to your own countries and others to forced exile. You can go proudly. You are history. You are legend. You are the heroic example of democracy's solidarity and universality.

We shall not forget you, and when the olive tree of peace puts forth its leaves again, entwined with the laurels of the Spanish republic's victory—come back!

Come back to us. With us those of you who have no country will find one, those of you who have to live deprived of friendship will find friends, and all of you will find the love and gratitude of the whole Spanish people who, now and in the future, will cry out with all their hearts.

Long live the heroes of the international brigades!

"The Final Review": Milt Wolff leading the brigade in its final review before returning home, October 16, 1938. Photo by Robert Capa

Notes:

1. Dave Mitchell, *The Spanish Civil War* (London, New York: Granada, 1982)
2. Milt Felsen, *The Anti-Warrior, A Memoir* (Iowa City: University of Iowa Press, 1980)
3. Peter N. Carroll, *The Odyssey of the Abraham Lincoln Brigade* (Stanford, Calif.: Stanford University Press, 1994)
4. *For Whom the Bell Tolls* was published by Scribner in 1940.
5. Tom Mooney was a San Francisco labor activist who was imprisoned for allegedly bombing a World War I Preparedness Day parade. It is commonly believed he was framed. The campaign to Free Tom Mooney became an international cause célèbre. He was finally released from prison in 1939 by Governor Culbert Olsen, who had promised to free Mooney if elected. Another International Brigade company was named after the socialist/communist organizer Mother Bloor.
6. Hugh Thomas, *The Spanish Civil War* (New York: Harper & Row, 1977)

The international brigades began withdrawing from Spain in November of 1938. On November 9, thousands of Jewish businesses, schools, and cemeteries were attacked in Germany in what came to be known as Kristallnacht, "the Night of Broken Glass." Thirty thousand Jews were arrested. Franco's forces overran Madrid four months later, in March of 1939. Six months after that, in September, Germany invaded Poland. World War II, the most devastating war in human history, began.

HOMECOMING

When the veterans of the Abraham Lincoln Brigade returned home, the Spanish civil war was ending, but their battle was just beginning. The United States government immediately seized their passports and threatened them with prosecution for violating the Neutrality Act. The Dies Committee (later the House Un-American Activities Committee, HUAC) formed in 1938 and began the congressional harassment of Spanish civil war vets and other progressives that would continue through the 1960s.

While the government harassed them, the vets received a hero's welcome from the Left. Their supporters overflowed Madison Square Garden. News stories of Hitler's army advancing on Europe and of the Nazis' persecution of Jews validated the vets' stand against fascism. They were treated like celebrities. "Our New Year's party was the hottest event in town," Wolff recalls.

Over six hundred thousand people died as a result of the Spanish civil war. Foreshadowing the behavior of fascist governments to come, Franco brutally repressed those who supported the Republic. Over one hundred thousand loyalist soldiers were executed, and two hundred thousand were imprisoned in Spain.

The war created a mass flight from Spain. Many of the internationals from countries like Germany, Poland, and Italy faced death if they returned to their former homes. Yet few found safe havens. The other European countries greeted them with hostility. Over two hundred thousand former loyalist soldiers were placed in concentration camps in France.[1] Volunteers who returned to the United States in one piece felt they had unfinished business and owed a debt to those who were left behind. Freedom for the Spanish prisoners and aid for the refugees

A rally for aid to Spanish refugees fills Madison Square Garden, 1945. *Peoples Weekly World*/Reference Center for Marxist Studies

became the new rallying point for the vets and their supporters.

"All the democracies betrayed these people. What did that say about the democracy I was brought up to think was so wonderful?" Hilda Roberts asks:

I had always been for the working people, but now it was an awakening to the true nature of my own government. When I came home, I started calling the president to lift the embargo. I thought Roosevelt was such a great guy, and now I had a different view. I joined the Communist Party, but I wasn't with it. I was too disillusioned with what was going on in the world, and the kids I met were too innocent and idealistic for what I just went through.

Like many of the other vets, Roberts joined the labor movement.

The vets had experienced not only the horrors of modern war and fascism, but also the conflict between idealism and reality. They experienced the seductive and the destructive power of organizations and comradery, the majesty of bravery and commitment, the corruption of

Relief Efforts

Social worker Virginia Malbin traveled to Spain as part of the National Social Workers Committee to Aid Spanish Democracy. Over one million Spanish people had been displaced by the bombing, and over sixty thousand children had become refugees. Malbin's task was to assess the situation of the refugee children and the effectiveness of relief efforts. She concluded that the Spanish social workers had set up an efficient network under the direction of Constancia de la Mora and were doing a good job, but they needed more resources. So Malbin suggested getting resources to the Spanish social workers rather than setting up a separate effort. Malbin worked with de la Mora in the Spanish government's heroic effort to care for the refugee children and to bring the entire peasant population up to a twentieth-century standard of living.

The main logistical problem was where to house those whose homes had been destroyed or who had been driven out by the advancing fascist armies. It made no sense to house them in areas that were under assault, so finally the Spanish started setting up group homes in monasteries and in the estates they had seized. This amazing story is told in de la Mora's autobiography, *In Place of Splendor.*

Malbin recalls, "In spite of the war and difficulties, I encountered more caring and concern for the welfare of Spanish children by the republican government than I encountered for the welfare of children as a social worker in the U.S. Before the revolution and the installation of a democratic government, the only Spanish schools were parochial schools. The Republic created the first public education system and a public health care system, right during the war. They were transforming the class of uneducated and poverty-stricken feudal peasants. What they did was educate the younger people and then give them the job of teaching the older people. It was exciting to see what people could do under dire and difficult circumstances. But the hopes for the democratic government and for freedom catalyzed ordinary people to do extraordinary things."

After Malbin's assessment of the refugee children's situation, she returned to the United States and went on a speaking tour to raise money for relief. She then went to Paris, where she worked with the International Relief Agency, which was receiving aid from other countries. She remembers opening a letter of support from Prime Minister Nehru of India while she worked there.

In 1938 Malbin returned to Spain to join her husband, Dr. Bernard Malbin, at the front to help with the evacuation of those in brigade hospitals. "I worked with the medical office to move people and Internationals to a safe situation. We had to get passports and make sure the wounded Internationals had a place to go. It was especially difficult for those from Germany, Italy, or Poland, because they couldn't go home. Much of Europe was dominated by the Nazis, and the French were putting refugees in concentration camps. We sent people to Latin America and Asia."

When Malbin came back to the United States, she continued to work to aid the Spanish refugees and also those who had been arrested by Franco in Spain. "After Franco won the war, there were mass arrests and persecutions," she explained. "We were trying to influence governments to pressure Franco and also to help the underground resistance in Spain."

"I spoke about Spain and got people to make political protests to our government and to raise money for refugees. You have to realize the world Depression was still going on, and we were still trying to get welfare for poor and unemployed Americans. But like always, those who had the least gave the most, and those who were wealthy gave the least. But you know that is how it is when you raise money."

How did she do it? "Well, when you are in your early twenties, you think you can do anything. And I was working with extremely well-organized people."

Almost seventy years later, Malbin barely shows her age. She still swims every day, goes river rafting, and travels widely.

Virginia Malbin, Oakland, 1997

organizational power, and the complexity of war. Those who survived both physically and mentally acquired the ability to navigate between idealism and pragmatism, and those skills would soon be put to the test.

The Hitler-Stalin Pact

Then came the Hitler-Stalin Pact, in which Adolf Hitler and Joseph Stalin agreed not to attack each other. The Nazis would be allowed to seize Poland, and in exchange, the Soviet Union was allowed to occupy Latvia, Lithuania, Estonia, and the eastern part of Poland. For many American communists, this was anathema, a pact with the devil. To liberals it was proof of what they had been saying all along, that communism was a form of tyranny, like Nazism. In response to the pact, many of the vets left both the Communist Party and their own veterans' group, the Veterans of the Abraham Lincoln Brigade (VALB).

To this day, many of the vets defend the pact as a purely pragmatic move on the part of the Soviets. Milt Wolff places it in the context of the Soviet Union's offer to the Czechoslovak government and to the Western powers to take a stand against Hitler's invasion of Czechoslovakia. The Western powers had made a pact with Germany; seeing the Soviet Union and communism as greater threats than Nazism, they hoped that Germany would invade the Soviet Union. According to Wolff, the Soviets did what all the other Western powers had done: they made a deal to save themselves by selling out other nations. One thing the pact certainly symbolizes is the end of any pretense of moral justification for the foreign policy of governments of any political stripe.

The vets dealt with this contradiction in different ways. Jack Shafran defied the Communist Party and VALB dictates and joined the U.S. Army. "I wanted to fight fascism," is his simple statement. He was castigated for enlisting and wearing his army uniform to a peace meeting. Not long after criticizing Shafran publicly for

Lincoln brigade vets marching against U.S. intervention in World War II prior to the invasion of the Soviet Union. *Peoples Weekly World*/Reference Center for Marxist Studies

Above: Jack Shafran in Spain. Harry Fisher personal collection

Left: Jack Shafran, New York, 1997

breaking discipline, Milt Wolff was approached by William J. ("Wild Bill") Donovan of the U.S. Office of Strategic Services (OSS, forerunner of the CIA). Donovan hooked Wolff up with British Intelligence, and Wolff began secretly recruiting European nationals to work with the partisan resistance fighters in German-occupied countries. In public he enforced the party line, but in private he followed his own conscience.

Judgment Day for Fascism? The U.S. Enters the War

Hitler invaded the Soviet Union in 1941, negating the Hitler-Stalin pact and bringing the Soviet Union into the war. Japan bombed Pearl Harbor, ending the U.S. attempt at isolation. Spanish civil war vets could now join forces with a worldwide movement to defeat fascism (even if it was an alliance by default on the part of the attacked).

The vets' efforts to fight were met with resistance. When they joined the U.S. Army, they were labeled "premature antifascists" and barred from becoming officers and from active duty in the European war theater. This discriminatory policy ended after a long campaign by VALB office manager Jack Bjoze that culminated in a demonstration in Washington. There Bjoze met with columnist Drew Pearson, who broke the story in the *Washington Post* in April of 1943.[2]

Bill Sennett and Jim Vogat at Kaider Field, Mississippi, 1943. From the author's collection

Hilda Roberts fared better than many. She served in the army as a nurse:

They knew I was in Spain. My commanding officer would brag about it. When people would say, "She must be a communist," he would say, "No, she can't be a communist."

But even so, she served in the Pacific theater, not in Europe:

I didn't like it. It wasn't like the Spanish army. The officers, especially from the South, were prejudiced against blacks and Jews. Everything seemed so superficial, how you salute your officer and like that.

Approximately four hundred and twenty-five Spanish civil war vets served in the U.S. armed forces during World War II, and another hundred were in the merchant marine. Some, including Irving Goff, Milt Felsen, Milt Wolff, and Al Tanz, worked with the OSS. Tanz was part of an elite group that parachuted into France in preparation for the D-Day invasion of Normandy. His mission was to cut electrical wires overlooking the beach where the Allied forces were to land. Later he participated in the liberation of Saint-Mère-Eglise, the first village liberated on D-Day, June 6, 1944. Tanz eventually attained the rank of captain in the U.S. Army and helped liberate the Nordhausen concentration camp in Germany. Herman Bottcher and

Above: Jack Bjoze in the 1960s. *Peoples Weekly World*/Reference Center for Marxist Studies

Left: Jack Bjoze, New York, 1997

Above: Al Tanz on a practice jump in preparation for parachuting into occupied France
to cut the German communication lines
before the D-Day invasion at Normandy.
Tanz private collection

Right: Al Tanz celebrating his ninetieth birth-
day, El Cerrito, California, 2000

Bob Thompson received distinguished service honors, and Edward Carter would later receive a medal of honor. As a paratrooper in the 101st Airborne, Saul Wellman helped liberate Holland and fought in the Battle of the Bulge. He was badly wounded and captured by the Germans but escaped and was hospitalized for six months.

Soon after the U.S. entered the war, Milt Wolff was approached by his old associate Bill Donovan to serve in the OSS, but wanting to see action, he refused and signed up for officers' training. When it was discovered that he had fought in Spain, he was kicked out of officers' training and then spent a good portion of the war transferring from command to command, trying to get to the front. When he finally got there, he was in Burma, not Europe. Wolff had never been wounded in Spain, but he was felled by a mosquito in Burma. While he was recovering from malaria, Donovan again contacted him, and Wolff joined the OSS. The war was nearly over by the time he finally made it to Europe.

Stationed in Italy, Wolff worked his old contacts who had served with the Garibaldi Battalion, the Italian equivalent of the Lincoln Battalion, in Spain. Then came the moment he had been waiting for. In northern Italy, he met a group of about thirty Spaniards who had been working with the Maquis, the French resistance. They were heading for Spain to join the resistance to Franco. Excited, he asked if there was any way he could help, and he forwarded their request for supplies to his commanding officer. "It was the biggest mistake of my life," Wolff states, shaking his head nearly sixty years later. He received a call and was immediately shipped back to the United States, along with Irving Goff and the other members of his OSS group. "They didn't want any leftist organizing in Europe. I blew the whistle on them. God knows what happened to those poor Spaniards." Then, after a moment's recollection:

I was pretty naive back then. You know who Franco's greatest allies were? It wasn't Hitler. It wasn't Mussolini. It was Chamberlain and Halifax. England had heavy investments in Spain, 40 percent of their foreign corporate investments, and Franco gave them assurances that he wouldn't nationalize them. They were happy to have his army in control, protecting them.

Notes
1. Thomas, *Spanish Civil War*
2. Peter N. Carroll, *The Volunteer*, December 2003

Battalion commanders Bob Thompson and Phil Detro (top, left, center) in Spain. Thompson received the Distinguished Service Honor in World War II and was sent to jail under the Smith Act during the McCarthy era. Tamiment Library, Abraham Lincoln Brigade Archives, New York University

THE GREAT WAR AGAINST FASCISM IS OVER; THE WAR HAS JUST BEGUN

A housewives' demonstration against the McCarthy-inspired witch hunts of the 1950s. *Peoples Weekly World/* Reference Center for Marxist Studies

Dave Smith was leaving the subway station for Flushing, New York, when two FBI agents walked up next to him. "Hello, Dave," one of them said. "How are you doing? We could use some help from guys like you. You are a patriotic guy, aren't you Dave?"

"Don't bother me," Smith replied.

"There's a lot of money here, Dave." Smith was unemployed at the time, and the agents offered him $25,000 if he would become an informant. He refused and was later called before the House Un-American Activities Committee.

World War II ended with the defeat of the Axis powers. Mussolini was hung by the Italian resistance, Hitler is alleged to have committed suicide, and the emperor of Japan surrendered. Franco was the last remaining fascist dictator. The Spanish people thought their hour was near; the Allies would finish the job and liberate them from Franco's iron grip. It never happened. Franco, although allied with Germany, had stayed out of the war and was allowed to remain in power and continue his brutal rule. Tens of thousands of people would be imprisoned, tortured, and killed in the thirty-six years of the Franco dictatorship, many buried in hidden graves.

The Spanish civil war vets returned to the United States from the Second World War with the same raison d'etre as when the war began, the overthrow of the Franco dictatorship and the release of prisoners in Franco's jails. The VALB would continue to appeal to the U.S. State Department to intervene in the execution and persecution of Spanish dissidents, and the vets would continue to demonstrate in front of the Spanish consulate in New York, demanding release of prisoners. Moe Fishman, who walked with a limp from an injury sustained in the battle of Brunete, and Dr. Edward Barsky, who had been in charge of the medical bureau in Spain, helped run the Joint Anti-Fascist Refugee Committee ("the Joint") to assist Spanish exiles.

With the end of the war against fascism, the Cold War between the United States and the Soviet Union began, and the United States used this as the basis for declaring war on progressives in the United States. The attorney general drew up a list of organizations labeled as subversive,

and the Lincoln vets were listed twice, once at the beginning (the Abraham Lincoln Brigade) and again near the end (the Veterans of the Abraham Lincoln Brigade).

As the House Un-American Activities Committee (HUAC) began their hearings, Joseph McCarthy began similar hearings in the Senate. People were called before these committees and charged with being members of or associated with the Communist Party. If they admitted they had knowledge of the party, they were forced, under threat of contempt charges and jail time, to name other people they knew in the party. Those named were then persecuted by the FBI, which often meant loss of their jobs and eviction from their homes. Their children were harassed and in some cases expelled from school. The FBI even visited nursery schools!

The Joint became a target of HUAC, and ten members of the group, including novelist Howard Fast, were sent to jail for three months for refusing to cooperate with the committee. Dr. Edward Barsky's medical license was suspended. The convictions were appealed to the U.S. Supreme Court, but the high court upheld them. Dissenting Justice William O. Douglas stated, "When a doctor cannot save lives in America because he is opposed to Franco in Spain, it is time to call a halt and look critically at the neurosis that has possessed us."

The most famous victims of HUAC were the Hollywood Ten, a group of high-profile Hollywood screenwriters, directors, and producers

Dr. Edward Barsky speaking on behalf of Spanish exiles. Tamiment Library, Abraham Lincoln Brigade Archives, New York University

Above: Alvah Bessie in Spain. Tamiment
Library, Abraham Lincoln Brigade Archives,
New York University, Veterans of the
Abraham Lincoln Brigade Photograph
Collection

Left: Alvah Bessie, one of the Hollywood Ten,
Oakland, 1985

who were sent to jail and blacklisted from working in the motion picture industry. The ten included Abraham Lincoln Brigade member Alvah Bessie.

Fred Keller, another Lincoln vet, was charged by HUAC with subverting the labor movement. Ten members of the Communist Party central committee, including Lincoln vets Bob Thompson and John Gates, were convicted under the Smith Act, which equated communism with sedition. They were sentenced to ten years in jail. While in jail, Thompson was badly beaten. Steve Nelson, Saul Wellman, and Bob Klonsky were convicted in subsequent trials. In 1955 the Veterans Administration canceled disability payments to veterans convicted under the Smith Act. Wellman, who had been seriously injured in World War II during the Battle of the Bulge, received a bill to repay over nine thousand dollars for treatment of his war injury.

The Smith Act convictions were later overturned by the U.S. Supreme Court, which ruled in 1957 that people could not be convicted for their beliefs. William Hundly, one of the prosecutors who brought the cases against Wellman and Nelson, later stated that the prosecutions were a mistake. However, the damage had been done. Communism had been delegitimized, equated with criminal activity in the minds of the uninformed public, and many lives were destroyed.

Nearly all the Spanish civil war vets tell stories of being visited by the FBI, and most lost jobs.

A Gold Watch to the FBI Man Who Followed Me for 25 Years
Ray Durem

Well, old spy
looks like I
led you down some pretty blind alleys,
took you on several trips to Mexico,
fishing in the high Sierras,
jazz at the Philharmonic.
You've watched me all your life,
I've clothed your wife,
put your two sons through college.
What good has it done?
Sun keeps rising every morning.
Ever see me buy an Assistant President?
or close a school?
or lend money to Somoza?
I bought some after-hours whiskey in L.A.
but the Chief got his pay.
I ain't killed no Koreans,
or fourteen-year-old boys in Mississippi,
neither did I bomb Guatemala,
or lend guns to shoot Algerians.
I admit I took a Negro child
to a white restroom in Texas,
but she was my daughter, only three,
and she had to pee,
and I just didn't know what to do,
would you?

Now, old FBI man,
you've done the best you can.
You lost me a few jobs,
scared a couple of landlords.
You got me struggling for that bread,
but I ain't dead.
And before it's all through
I may be following you!

Helen Freeman with Fred Keller, Oakland, 1986. Keller was charged by HUAC with subverting the labor movement

Left: Bob Klonsky, Oakland, 1989

Below: Pennsylvania Smith Act defendants, including Bob Klonsky, top left. Klonsky would later become active as a lawyer in civil rights cases. *Peoples Weekly World*/Reference Center for Marxist Studies

Sana Goldblatt at her home in San Francisco, 1998. Goldblatt was hounded by the FBI during the McCarthy era and forced to move from job to job until she finally moved to San Francisco and began working as an occupational therapist for the Jewish Home for the Aged in the mid-1950s. Her employer refused to cooperate with the FBI. "Now that I knew I didn't have to worry about keeping a job," she says, "I started going to demonstrations again and became active in the Women's League for Peace and Freedom." She was one of the founders of the Bay Area VALB post.

A Prosecutor's Apology

Those who look back at their participation in the Communist Party with misgivings are not the only ones to regret too closely following the dictates of a party line. Smith Act prosecutor William Hundley succeeded in obtaining convictions against Saul Wellman and Steve Nelson, sending them both to jail. In 1999 Judy Montell, working on a film about Saul Wellman, interviewed Hundley to hear from the other side. During the interview he apologized. The following is an edited version of his remarks:

"The trial was during the McCarthy era, and the country was virulently anticommunist, and the Communist Party was feared. We reviewed all of the informant's written reports to the FBI and they would be talking endlessly about civil rights; they would be talking about the poor; they'd be talking about unemployment; or they would be talking about socialism being better than capitalism. Whether you like that or not, it's certainly perfectly legal. We were charging them with conspiring to advocate the overthrow of the government. Finally I came across, in one of these reports—and it's unusual, they're talking about the unions or something—and some guy stands up at the meeting and says, 'Let's cut out all this nonsense. When are we gonna start the revolution?'

"So I'm a young lawyer. I get all excited. That's the kind of evidence I need to use at the trial. So I go to the FBI and say, 'I want that.' And they all huddle and they come back and they say, 'Listen, Bill—you can't have that, because that guy who jumped up at the meeting is one of our informants.'

"At one point, for security, the American Communist Party broke down into cells of three, so they would only know the others in their cell. I find out that in each cell of three, there were probably two FBI informants. We had a couple in the trial that were not only FBI informants, they were informants for the Ford Motor Company about the union. Now, when that came out, in a normal case, it probably would have killed the prosecution. But not in 1953 when we were trying a bunch of admitted Communist Party functionaries.

"Saul, I'm sorry I prosecuted you. I'm sorry you had to go through that. I never totally agreed with your views. I thought a lot of them were way out. But they certainly didn't deserve to be prosecuted, and you to spend time in jail. If there's any one individual in my opinion who was responsible for these trials, it was J. Edgar Hoover. He pushed them. But eventually everybody came to their senses. All of the convictions were reversed, and should have been reversed. But in the meantime these people spent time in jail. I think we all lost our ability to tolerate dissent in that period. Fortunately we got it back. I prosecuted a lot of cases in my career, and these are the only ones I regret. With everything else I have no problems."

Many were forced to find new careers, and many left the country. Lincoln Brigade nurse Lini Fuhr was fired from one job after another as the FBI followed her around the country. Finally she moved to Mexico, where she helped set up a rural health system.

Descent to the Underground

After the arrest of the Communist Party central committee in the U.S., the party leadership feared mass arrests similar to what had happened in Nazi Germany before the war, or in the United States during the 1920s Palmer Raids, when thousands of immigrants were rounded up and deported. The party ordered several hundred of its top leaders to hide from the government by going "underground." Those who went underground disappeared. They left their families and moved to other towns and assumed new identities. "They asked me to go," recalls Dave Smith:

I went underground for two years. That was the worst mistake of my life. I couldn't do any organizing, and that was my whole life. It was crazy. How can you have an underground movement? The population has to be behind you to protect you. I was supposed to be the backup leadership for Queens and Suffolk Counties, but all I did was work in an auto parts place. Our party group would meet every once in a while, and finally we bought a car between us and went to athletic events.

It was hard on the families of those who went underground. Archie Brown lived underground for five years, during which he rarely saw his wife, Esther "Hon" Brown. She was left to take care of their four kids with help from her parents. Hon Brown had wanted to be a truck driver in Spain, but the leadership refused her because she was a woman. Later she became the secretary of the San Francisco Bay Area VALB.

Dave Smith's wife, Sofie, was having a difficult time while he was underground. Ironically, she was saved by FBI agents who paid a visit to her Italian neighbors. The agents had hoped to turn them into informants, but instead, the neighbors threw the agents out and then knocked on Sofie's door offering their assistance. "They really took care of her like she was one of their own. She became part of their family," Dave Smith recalls. "They were really nice people. I think they were in the Mafia."

Abe Osheroff was tipped off by a friend that he was about to be arrested. He went underground but missed his party contact, who was supposed to provide money and help in setting up a new identity. To support himself while underground, Osheroff did a variety of jobs, including writing theses for college students. Later he became a carpenter. "Carpentry gave me some independence," he states. Years later, after he surfaced, he was working on a carpentry job

They stopped me on street corners. They came up to me on buses. They went to all my employers....At least once a month, sometimes once every other day, but very often at least once a week for fifteen years the FBI came and threatened me. I tried to keep my cool during that whole period, but it was hard. I told them, "You want to talk about me, fine. I will talk about me. But I will not say anything about anybody else." They didn't want to know anything about me. I guess they knew. They knew I wasn't a member of the Communist Party. They knew I was just an antifascist, that I went to Spain to fight the Italian fascists, the kind of Italians that had made my father run away from his country. But they wouldn't let me alone. I felt like I was under house arrest. I did manage to get married, but it was relatively late, when things were over, when I could risk going out and meeting people. But let me tell you, I would do everything over again. I would do exactly the same thing.

—*Rosario Pistone, in* The Premature Antifascists: North American Volunteers in the Spanish Civil War, 1936–39, *by John Gerassi*

Martin Balter, New York, 2001. To avoid being blacklisted, he took his mother's maiden name.

when FBI agents walked onto the job site and approached his boss. He figured he was about to get fired. After they had left, he went to talk to the boss, who turned to him and said, "Abe, those guys in suits told me you're a communist. I told them I didn't know anything about communists, but if they all work as hard as Abe, I'll hire every one they send me."

Assault on the Labor Movement

Many believe that the real targets of HUAC and McCarthy were not the communists but the New Deal Democrats and labor. The conservatives wanted to put a halt to social services programs passed under Franklin Roosevelt, such as social security, unemployment insurance, and the right of workers to join unions. They wanted to reverse the role of government from protecting the welfare of working people and consumers to promoting big business, as had been the case under previous administrations.

Before the progressive legislation passed during the New Deal, it was common practice for employers to demand that their employees work as many hours per day as the employers wanted, subject them to unsafe working conditions, pay them inadequately, and fire them without justification. Sexual harassment and racism were taken for granted. If workers objected or tried to organize into unions, the employers could hire private armies, such as the Pinkertons, to terrorize them. Jobs were scarce and there was no safety net for the unemployed. If a family was behind on its rent, a landlord could hire private security agents to come into the apartment and throw the family and their belongings out onto the street. The only social services or welfare programs were provided by religious organizations or fraternal orders, such as the Jewish immigrants' Workmen's Circle.

The Democratic Party and the progressive movement succeeded in getting legislation passed that gave workers the right to join unions, such protections as the eight-hour workday and forty-hour work week, the right to fair employment practices, and unemployment insurance. The Communist Party provided the organizational structure to turn out large numbers of people to demonstrate, and it helped articulate and popularize a progressive ideology. It had a unified program and agenda that cut across all sectors of society. It romanticized the trade union movement and its members were key union organizers. However, Communist Party support became a mixed blessing. Because the American Communist Party was aligned with the Soviet Union, it was easy for conservatives to label it un-American. Business interests could then use the Communist label to attack reforms. One of their main targets was the union movement, as it directly challenged the power of employers at the workplace.

The Taft-Hartley Act, passed in 1947, was the beginning of postwar legislation aimed at turning back the gains made by the labor movement during the New Deal era. The bill restricted the rights of labor unions to organize, strike, and take political action. One provision required union officials to sign affidavits stating that none of their officers were communists. President Truman vetoed the bill, but his veto was overridden. The Communist Control Act went even farther, making it a crime for communists to hold union office. Both the organizers and rank-and-filers who had been the heart and soul of labor were purged from the movement they had helped build. A few unions, like the International Longshore and Warehouse Union (ILWU) and the United Electrical Workers, refused to knuckle under, and they became safe havens for labor's political refugees, including many Lincoln Brigade vets, among them Bill Bailey, George Kaye, Nate Thornton, Leonard Olson, and Luchelle McDaniels.

ILWU executive board member and Lincoln vet Archie Brown challenged the anticommunist labor laws, publicly stating, after being elected to the board, that he was a communist. Arrested in 1961 for taking his stand, he fought all the way to the U.S. Supreme Court. His attorneys argued that he was being persecuted for his beliefs, not his actions, the same way people were tried for treason because of their religious beliefs during feudal times. In 1964, in *United States v. Brown,* the U.S. Supreme Court agreed with Brown and declared the ban on communist labor leadership unconstitutional.

Brown later led the ILWU in its refusal to unload cargo ships from Chile, in protest of Pinochet's military coup, and in its boycott of ships from South Africa, which helped launch the worldwide anti-apartheid boycott.

Bill Bailey, Oakland, 1982

Above: Steve Nelson, c. 1936. Tamiment
Library, Abraham Lincoln Brigade Archives,
New York University

Right: Steve Nelson, 1989

Khrushchev Revelations: Keeping a Moral Compass when the Earth Crumbles

Critics of the veterans of the Lincoln Brigade and the VALB organization have often labeled them pawns of the Communist Party. The majority of the vets considered themselves anti-fascist fighters, driven by the ideals of socialism and communism. Although he identifies with the values of communism, Milt Wolff, in testifying to congressional committees, often denied membership in the Communist Party. Abraham Lincoln Brigade Archive historian Peter Carroll, after extensive interviews and research, found no indication that the Communist Party directly influenced the VALB organization. However, the number of vets who were in high leadership positions in the party is significant. Having fought in Spain gave them status, and their war experience increased their leadership abilities. Harassment by the FBI increased their doubts about the sincerity of the U.S. government's commitment to democracy. However, by the mid-1950s, most vets who had been members had left the party, although many still believed that the communist Soviet Union offered a humanistic alternative to the problems of capitalism, a view that was to be shattered. And as in other crises, the vets proved their ability to act according to their consciences.

In 1956 the new Soviet premier, Nikita Khrushchev, revealed to the world the atrocities committed by his predecessor: Joseph Stalin had run the country with a reign of terror, murdering millions of people, suppressing any challenge to his rule.

"There are no more gods," Steve Nelson stated in disbelief. He was chairing the meeting of the American Communist Party where Khrushchev's speech was first announced. "This is not the reason I joined the Communist Party. From now on we have to reject this; we have to make our own decisions," he concluded.[1]

The revelation sent shock waves through the Veterans of the Abraham Lincoln Brigade. The vets had survived two wars and blacklisting, and some had been to jail, but the revelations about the totalitarian nature of the Soviet Communist Party, of which the American Communist Party was an affiliate, caused progressives—whether party members or not—to question their very reason for being.

Steve Nelson reading the *Daily Worker* while on trial under the Smith Act. "There are no more gods," he responded to the Khrushchev revelations. *Peoples Weekly World*/Reference Center for Marxist Studies

Communist Party organizer Abe Osheroff responded by publicly resigning from the CP and suggesting that the vets turn their publication, *The Volunteer,* into a forum for debating and denouncing the party. Milt Wolff disagreed and was labeled a Stalinist. "I just wanted to keep *The Volunteer* as a publication for the vets," he states today. Nelson, who had been a commissar in Spain and had served time in jail for sedition, became part of the VALB faction that left the party. After a tumultuous struggle about the future of VALB, Nelson replaced Wolff as head of VALB's New York office.

After being replaced, Milt Wolff moved to California and moved in with Frieda, the woman he describes as the love of his life, also a political activist. He became commander of the Bay Area post of VALB. His statement about wanting to keep *The Volunteer* for the vets in many ways sums up his goals. The veterans and the Spanish civil war are his lifelong cause, and he used VALB and its prestige to do as much good as he

Abe Osheroff working as a party organizer in 1941. He would vehemently renounce the party after the Khrushchev revelations, but he continued a life of political activism and involvement in radical politics.

could for other causes. One of the organization's main functions in later years has been to use its yearly reunions to raise money for other causes, which they have done with legendary success.

Wolff's response to the Khrushchev revelations and his ability to shrug off the Communist Party's failings may have to do with his relationship to the party. For Wolff, as for most of the Lincoln vets, the Communist Party was a vehicle that could be used to do good things in the world. The battle was to keep some independence, and like all relationships, it was based on compromise. He was always his own man, if anything to a fault. He had his own organization, the VALB, and didn't need the party to function politically. But since he was not under CP discipline, he may not have had the same feeling of betrayal as those who were; their feelings of responsibility and regret may account for the dramatic trajectory of their relationship to the party.

The Soviet Union's invasion of Hungary a few months after Khrushchev's speech was the last straw for many of those who had remained in the party until that point. Lincoln vet John Gates, editor of the party's national publication, the *Daily Worker,* ran editorials critical of the Soviet Union's invasion and soon left the party. He had been one of the top Communist Party leaders convicted and sent to jail under the Smith Act. After going back to school, he went to work for the International Ladies Garment Workers Union, led by anticommunist David Dubinsky. Gates eventually denounced communism and became a liberal Democrat, supporting President Johnson's Great Society programs and the Vietnam War.[2]

The U.S. Communist Party claimed a membership of seventy-five thousand in 1945. By the time of Khrushchev's revelations, a decade of harassment by HUAC had reduced the number to seventeen thousand. By the end of 1956, less than five thousand remained, and of those a significant number were FBI agents and informants.

Osheroff was one of the most bitterly outspoken against the party. His doubts had begun during the Spanish civil war. One of the men that he had brought over fell apart under the pressure of combat, and Osheroff asked the commissar, Joe Dallet, to send the man to Barcelona for medical help. Dallet took this as a sign of discontent and a challenge to his leadership. Max Shufer told Osheroff that Dallet was planning to set him up to be killed in action. "I was scared shitless," Osheroff recalls. "And I shared my feeling with the neighborhood guys." Dallet, the son of a wealthy New England family, affected a phony working-class accent, and the rank and file did not enjoy having him boss them around. A couple of the "guys" told Osheroff that they paid Dallet a visit. They had reminded him that they were from the other side of the tracks. Then they handed Dallet a bullet and let him know that if anything happened to Osheroff, the next one he got would be in the back of his head. After the meeting, Dallet approached Osheroff and told him to be careful and to stay in the back and not take any chances.

Although arrogant, Dallet had some integrity. Feeling pressured to prove himself to the working-class men he was attempting to command, during the following action he went over the top to rescue a wounded soldier. He was killed by enemy fire.

"I learned that people in the cause were less than perfect," Osheroff reflects:

The cause can be all screwed up. There was no way we could win without the aid of France and England—but to talk about it could be considered treason....I was pretty naive then. I thought the problems with the party would be self-correcting, but then later I realized the problems were with the party itself. I was raised in a radical humanist tradition, in a neighborhood where if the landlord put out a neighbor's furniture on the street, we would put it back inside. I found a home in the Communist Party. When I began to think and act radically, the Communist Party was my family, and no matter what the problems were, they were still family. But then you find out father is a pimp and mother is a whore, and you realize that you need to find a new family.

The years of persecution had created a siege mentality, an us-versus-them feeling. Many of those who left the party were reluctant to criticize it in public and were critical of those who did. Ruth Davidow felt she could no longer be politically effective, given the turmoil and battles for leadership, as well as the growing conflict between China and Russia. She kept her beliefs and continued to fight for her ideals, but separately from the Communist Party USA. Her words exemplify the beliefs of many others:

I do not want to put my time into the party to correct it, so I therefore don't want to attack it either. I think that when you make a criticism you should be prepared to work on it, and I'm not....The party has given leadership to every progressive struggle in this country since I've been around. It has always been in the forefront on the question of discrimination and on the question of support to any progressive movement. Now, methodology is something else. I still support the party, but I'm not in it. I just can't take their tactics. There are certain types of people who need that kind of leadership or demand it. I find it stifling. I don't need someone in an office downtown to analyze things for me, I can take action on my own.[5]

By the time of the Khrushchev revelations, Dave Smith had already left the party. "I was a working-class guy and that was where my ambitions were—to organize the working class." After the war he became a machinist and then he got a job in a large factory, where he worked as a rank-and-file organizer for the United Electrical Workers Union. Perhaps his thoughts sum up the experience of most of the vets and their relationship to communism and the party:

The party did a lot of good work in this country because people believed they were involved in a bigger struggle and went along with it. The idea of building a better society overrode everything else. What other options were there during the Depression and afterwards? The party had hundreds of thousands of members at the time, but then people left, scared, and also disillusioned with some of the decisions to support everything the Soviet Union did.

A combination of FBI harassment and the injury to his arm in Spain later forced Smith to give up his career as a machinist. He went back to school and became a biology teacher. He organized a union at the high school where he worked and became active in the American Federation of Teachers. After he retired, he moved to a small community in Vermont to live near the woods. He and his wife became active in local politics and the environmental movement, serving on the town council and nature conservancies, working for laws to protect forests from development and acid rain. Vermont Governor Madeleine Kunin once referred to Dave and Sofie Smith as "the conscience of Vermont."

Above: Archie Brown was ejected from HUAC hearings in San Francisco three times. 1960, *San Francisco Chronicle*.

Left: Archie Brown, Oakland, 1982

The Left Strikes Back

In 1960, HUAC came to San Francisco expecting to intimidate those called before it, as it had done for a decade. But this time they were met with defiance. Archie Brown, who had been called to testify, denounced the committee and was ejected from the hearing three times, once being dragged out screaming, "Go home!" The media ran pictures of student demonstrators being beaten and washed down the steps of San Francisco City Hall with fire hoses, in scenes resembling the treatment of civil rights protestors in the South. Vets Ruth Davidow and Vernon Brown were arrested for disturbing the peace. As it had turned out, Madrid was not "the tomb of fascism," but the San Francisco hearings were the beginning of the end for HUAC. The demonstrations also marked the beginning of the student free speech movement and a new era of progressive politics.

Notes
1. Maurice Isserman, *Which Side Were You On?* (Urbana: University of Illinois, 1993)
2. Peter N. Carroll, interview with John Gates, 1990
3. Montell, *Forever Activists*

THE PARTY'S OVER; THE PARTY HAS JUST BEGUN

The Civil Rights Movement

Racial equality was a goal of the Abraham Lincoln Brigade from its inception. The brigade was the first integrated fighting unit of Americans, and Lincoln Brigade commander Oliver Law was one of the first African Americans to command white troops. Many of the blacks who served in Spain saw defending the Republic as an extension of the fight against segregation and the Ku Klux Klan. African American vet Jimmy Yates, one of almost a hundred African Americans to serve in Spain, titled his autobiography *Mississippi to Madrid.*[1] Paul Robeson, probably the most famous black performing artist of the time, toured the troops, as did the poet Langston Hughes.

Black and white vets who went on to serve during World War II were disappointed to find that the racial equality they had experienced in the Spanish army did not exist in the American military. Luchelle McDaniels challenged the segregation of a lunch counter at Woolworth's in South Africa, foreshadowing events that would take place in the United States twenty years later.

After the war, the vets continued to make contributions to the civil rights struggle. Milt Wolff went to work for the Civil Rights Congress, touring the South with a black folk singer in defense of several black people falsely accused of crimes. Vet John Penrod demonstrated with sit-down strikers to integrate lunch counters in Gainesville, Florida.

A major problem in the 1950s and 1960s was the outright refusal of landlords in many white neighborhoods to rent to people of color. In

John Penrod, New York, 1999

Above: Luchelle McDaniels (right) in Spain. Tamiment Library, Abraham Lincoln Brigade Archives, New York University

Right: Luchelle McDaniels at a senior power demonstration in Sacramento, 1982

Lillian and Buster Ross, Oakland, 1988. The Rosses fought to integrate the Levittown housing projects.

1947, Buster Ross and his wife, Lillian, moved into a segregated housing development in Levittown, Long Island. They invited some black friends to stay with them and were promptly served with eviction orders. Lincoln vet and union organizer Ross went into action, gaining the support of local politicians, labor officials, and even baseball star Jackie Robinson. Eventually Levittown was desegregated.[2]

After one of the housing committees Davidow worked with scored a victory, the Democratic Party became interested in working with the group. However, during an election of officers, a representative from the party raised an objection to Davidow's nomination. "Before we do any nominations, I'd like to tell you that I have heard that Ruth Davidow is a dangerous communist," she remembers him saying. She describes the group's reaction:

The place was thunderstruck. Everybody looked at me, and I said, "Well, I don't respond to accusations of that kind. I'm going to tell you what I do, and if that makes me a communist, then I'm a communist and that's fine with me." And I went through the whole history of the housing fight, the integration fight, discrimination fights, and all the other things that I was active in that made the FBI come around and accuse me of being a communist. I had barely sat down when the minister got up and said, "If she's a communist, I'm a communist, because I believe in everything she said and everything she did!" And when he sat

down, somebody else got up, and by the time we were through, practically everybody in that room had stood up and said the same thing. So I have great faith in people, especially if they know you and really understand what you're doing.[3]

Davidow's real passions were public health and Head Start, the program for providing education, health services, and nutritional services to preschool children. She offered to help the Student Nonviolent Coordinating Committee (SNCC) recruit someone to work on Head Start in the South. Civil rights workers had been beaten up and even murdered. It was a hard sell. When she failed to find someone else to go, she went herself. She began working in a Head Start program in Mississippi in 1966, training African Americans in health education and advocacy. She succeeded in persuading the state's health department to provide vaccinations to fifteen hundred rural children. "It was a really fabulous job we did that summer. What we left was even more important. We left a group of young workers who all felt like professionals," she states.[4]

After Mississippi, Davidow helped set up a health clinic in San Francisco's Haight-Ashbury district to treat children suffering from drug addiction. When Native Americans occupied Alcatraz Island for seventeen months in 1969 through 1971, they asked Davidow to provide medical care. One of the few non-Indians to live on the island during the occupation, she spent a year there. In the 1980s she took up the cause of

"I can't live in the world if I can't fight against injustice."

Ruth Davidow, Oakland, 1996

Bill Sennett (center) demonstrating against the Ku Klux Klan in Chicago, 1946. From the author's collection

homeless people and helped organize a union for the homeless. She eventually turned to film-making and produced twenty-one films about health care and political activism.

The Lincoln vet identified most with the civil rights movement is Abe Osheroff. Recovering from his falling out with the party and the knocks he took during the McCarthy period, Osheroff found his calling during what came to be known as Mississippi Freedom Summer. In Spain he had never had the opportunity to spend time with the Spanish people, as had many of the vets. In the South he was able to experience the lives of the people he was organizing and bond with them.

Through literacy tests and intimidation, African Americans in the South had been effectively denied the right to vote. In the summer of 1964, SNCC organized college students to go to the South to help register black people to vote. The students were met with violence; three were kidnapped and killed.

"I felt it wasn't enough to just raise money for SNCC. I needed to put my life on the line," Osheroff states. He went to Holmes County, Mississippi, to use his skills as a carpenter to build a community center in the town of Mileston. SNCC put him up with Hartman Turnbow, the first black person to register to vote in Mississippi since Reconstruction. When white vigilantes responded by firebombing his house, Turnbow ran outside, gun in hand, and badly wounded one of the night riders, a deputy sheriff. Reflecting on the experience, Osheroff says:

I learned more, living in that home with a black family, eating with them, and sharing their lives, than in all the years of reading as a leftist. The only other white person in town was the sheriff. I can remember at least twenty nighttime attacks where we had to come out of the house shooting. I was more scared than in Spain, even though the chances of getting hurt were much less.

Above: Abe Osheroff (center) stayed in the home of Hartman Turnbow in 1964 during Mississippi Freedom Summer. There they would have to defend themselves from the Ku Klux Klan. Photo by Matt Herron

Left: Abe Osheroff, New York, 1997

Leonard Olson with daughter Martha Olson Jarocki, Oakland, 1994. Martha was active in Mississippi Freedom Summer. For many of the vets' children, the civil rights movement and opposition to the war in Vietnam were their Spain.

Turnbow paid Osheroff the greatest compliment: "Damn, Abe, in your heart, you're a nigger just like me," he told him after one of the shootouts.

Ruth Davidow's and Abe Osheroff's reputations as Lincoln Brigade vets became part of the lore of the civil rights movement and inspired young civil rights workers. Michael Schwerner, one of the three white students killed in Mississippi in 1964, was the nephew of vet Murray Schwerner. Vet Leonard Olson's daughter Martha also went to Mississippi. "I was filled with pride to hear someone who fought in Spain was building a community center in Mileston," she stated. For Martha Olson-Jarocki and the other relatives of vets who joined SNCC in the South, Mississippi was their Spain.

Opposing the Vietnam War

In October 1967, seventy-five Lincoln vets marched behind the VALB banner during the historic March on the Pentagon. Over half a million people participated in this demonstration against the war in Vietnam. The VALB contingent chanted, "How many Guernicas, LBJ, will your bombers destroy in Vietnam today?"[5] The reception the Lincoln vets received made it evident that they had inspired new generations of activists. Moe Fishman, VALB office manager, described it:

Word spread that the Lincoln Brigade was coming, and a path opened up through the crowd as if by magic. To the applause of many of the young people present, we made our way in a single file. We got flowers and kisses.

The Vietnam War marked a turning point. The Spanish civil war vets had taken up arms to defend the Spanish democracy, hoping that the United States and its allies would intervene. But from Vietnam on, the VALB found themselves most often in opposition to U.S. intervention in other countries, from Southeast Asia to Latin America and later the Middle East.

History professor and Lincoln vet Robert Colodny explained the paradox of going to fight in Spain but opposing the fighting in Vietnam. Addressing a group of students after screening the French documentary *To Die in Madrid*, he said:

Men fought in Spain for more than the Republic, they fought for peace....If you have tears to shed for the million dead of the Spanish Republic, save them. Shed them for the million dead of Vietnam. And if you feel moved to praise the courage of the defenders of Madrid, save that praise too. Save it for the young men of your own generation who share with you the agony of Vietnam and who resist the war.

Robert Colodny speaking out against the war in Vietnam, c. 1967. Roby Newman private collection

Above: Chuck and Yolanda (Bobbie) Hall at a pre-Vietnam antiwar demonstration in Chicago in the 1950s opposing the nuclear arms race. Bobbie Hall was called before HUAC in Chicago in 1965, along with Lincoln vet Milt Cohn. She later ran the Chicago VALB chapter. Photo by Syd Harris from Mark Harris personal collection

Right: Chuck Hall, New York, 2001

Above: The Lincoln vets at the March on the Pentagon, 1967. Photo by Ted Reid, *Peoples Weekly World*/Reference Center for Marxist Studies

Left: Moe Fishman, New York, 1999

the Vietnam war. Colodny became a prominent social theorist. Besides an antiwar pamphlet, "Spain and Vietnam," published by the VALB, he is the author and editor of several academic works on philosophy, history, and science.

Maury Colow, a veteran of the Spanish civil war and World War II, used his organizational skills to help create Veterans for Peace. Marching in rallies against the Vietnam War, World War II vets wore their uniforms to combat the accusation of the right-wing Veterans of Foreign Wars that it was unpatriotic to oppose the Vietnam War. One day while he was working the desk at the Veterans for Peace office, two young Vietnam veterans walked in asking to help. He took them under his wing and helped them create their own organization; with some seed money from Veterans for Peace, the Vietnam Veterans Against the War got their start. VVAW would become one of the most significant organizations opposing the war in Vietnam.

Vets protesting the Vietnam War in San Francisco in the late 1960s. The Bancroft Library, University of California

Colodny received a doctorate in history from the University of California at Berkeley but was fired from his position as a teaching assistant in 1950 and blacklisted. When applying for other positions, he discovered that his school transcripts contained not only his grades, but also his FBI files, which included false accusations. The government continued to harass him for over a decade, calling him before committees and even threatening some of his students.[6] In the 1960s he toured U.S. communities, speaking out against

Ronald Reagan and the Call to Arms

Just as the people of Spain voted to come out of the Dark Ages, so have the people of Nicaragua. We went to Spain to stop the aggressors and avert World War II. And we were right. We could have stopped them in Spain. And what happened in Spain is happening in Central America. Once

again we've got to stop the aggressor. Only this time, we are the aggressors.
—Milt Wolff, referring to U.S. funding of the Contra mercenaries in Nicaragua

Crowds of demonstrators shouting *"No pasarán"* were again marching through the streets, this time in the 1980s, protesting U.S. activities in Central America. Nicaragua was one of the poorest countries in Latin America. Half the population was illiterate and earned less than three hundred dollars per year. Life expectancy was less than fifty-three years, and the infant mortality rate was 12 percent.[7] In July of 1979, the brutal dictator Anastasio Somoza was overthrown by a popular insurrection led by the Sandinistas, ending nearly half a century of tyranny. The Sandinista government launched a successful literacy campaign, built health clinics and housing, and instituted land reform. The Nicaraguan economy started growing and the population was rising out of poverty.

In 1981 Ronald Reagan became president of the United States. As part of his general anticommunist offensive, he cut off all U.S. aid to Nicaragua, citing the Sandinistas' Marxist ideology. He directed the CIA to organize and finance an army of mercenaries made up of Somoza's national guard to wage war against the Nicaraguan government.[8] An international solidarity movement formed to defend the new government against these mercenaries known as Contras, adopting the Spanish civil war slogan *"No pasarán."*

Reagan defended U.S. support of the Contras by stating that Americans have always fought in other wars, offering the example of the Lincoln Brigade. Then he added that the only problem with the Lincoln Brigade was that they had fought on the wrong side. The vets responded as if he had thrown down a gauntlet.

Applied physics professor and Lincoln Brigade vet Ted Veltfort, who had toured Nicaragua to advise the Sandinistas on restoring the country's damaged television system, wanted to help the victims of Contra attacks, who were often civilian populations of remote villages. Upon returning to the United States, he suggested VALB raise money to send ambulances to Nicaragua, as the veterans and their supporters had done in Spain. (Veltfort had driven an ambulance during the Spanish civil war.) VALB started with the goal of two ambulances. At their annual San Francisco Bay Area event, Milt Wolff stood in front of a cardboard ambulance and thermometer to indicate how much money they had raised and began his fund-raising pitch. By the time he was done, they were over the top of the thermometer. The vets had similar results at their events all over the country. They ended up raising enough money to send not two ambulances, but twenty. The astounding success of the ambulance drive amazed other groups on the Left and added to their admiration of the vets. In addition to sending ambulances, VALB also raised money for hospital generators and wheelchairs for the people of Nicaragua, El Salvador, and Cuba.

Ruth Davidow (center) at a San Francisco demonstration against U.S. involvement in Nicaragua, 1986. Photo by Richard Bermack

Above: Anthony Toney (right) marching in a demonstration in New York in the 1980s, opposing U.S. intervention in Latin America. Photo by Robert Coane

Right: Anthony Toney, Oakland, 1997

Not content just to give money, other vets contributed in various ways. Abe Osheroff put together a crew of carpenters, including his two sons, and headed for Nicaragua. They constructed fifty homes in a remote area. Before going, he raised $70,000 for supplies, which they shipped through Canada. Hilda Roberts made repeated trips to Nicaragua with the group Elders for Survival and housed activists who were on speaking tours about U.S. intervention in the Central American wars. Bob Reed helped establish a sister-city relationship between Seattle and Managua. Dave Smith got his small town of Bennington, Vermont, to adopt the sister city of Somotillo:

We had a broad range of people involved: bankers, teachers, Catholics, Methodists, Rotarians. We even had Republicans. We would go down [to Somotillo] in groups of six. It's still going on today.[9]

The effectiveness of the vets' assistance was recognized during a congressional hearing on Nicaragua. One of the Contra leaders defended U.S. intervention in Nicaragua by counterpoising it with the support that the Nicaraguan government was getting from "the old guys." He was referring to the Lincoln vets.

Cuba

The relationship between Lincoln vets and Cuba goes back to just after the Cuban revolution,

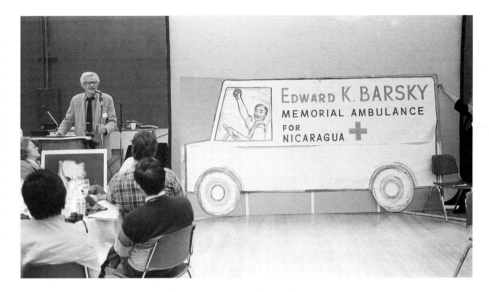

Milt Wolff at the 1985 Bay Area VALB reunion, raising money to send ambulances to Nicaragua. Photo by Richard Bermack

when vet Ted Veltfort and his family moved there. Veltfort had received an advanced degree in applied physics in the United States but was blacklisted for many years. Finally he landed a job, but after a few good years, his employer's company was sold. The new owners wanted Veltfort to design a communications system for use during a nuclear war. At that moment the new government of Cuba offered him a position teaching physics, and he seized the opportunity:

The best thing about Cuba at the time was seeing socialism working. It was a very human kind of socialism we could be happy with. We got to see socialism working in housing, health care, and education. Our three children all got excellent schooling. The health care was free and they had

Above: Veterans of the Abraham Lincoln Brigade in Nicaragua, in front of one of the ambulances they took with them. Vets include Martin Balter and Maury Colow (standing on the left), Saul Wellman, seated next to Archie Brown (wearing a cap), Milt Wolff, Al Gottlieb, Rudy Corbin, and Gabby Rosenstein (all standing). Photo by David Wills, 1986

Right: Milt Felsen in Cuba, 1993

some of the best doctors in the world. Before the revolution, only people with money could afford doctors.

The Veltforts' willingness to stand with the Cuban people during the Cuban missile crisis strengthened their sense of community. They felt especially good about raising their kids in a society relatively free from racism. The school system was completely integrated and their children learned from both black and white teachers. There was none of the racial tension and violence that was prevalent in the United States at the time, where the National Guard had to be called out to enable black children to attend white schools in the South.

In Cuba, the Veltforts found themselves living in a community of expatriate scientists and intellectuals from all over the world. Lenore Veltfort freelanced as a journalist. Besides teaching at the university, Ted helped the new country set up a center for solid-state electronics, where they produced the first solid-state semiconductors in Latin America.

The prerevolution Batista government had been known for its corruption. American Mafia dons controlled the casinos and nightclubs that symbolized Cuba's degradation and colonial relationship to the United States. Under the new government, the Veltforts experienced something similar to what several of the vets had found: they watched people who had suffered for generations finally being treated with dignity.

They recall a woman who worked for them as a maid. She had originally arrived in Cuba as a young orphan from Spain. "The nuns took care of orphans, but all they did was train them as domestic servants," Lenore Veltfort recalls:

By the time the revolution came, she was sixty years old. She was given her first opportunity to learn to read and write. She was so happy. She had lived in a rented room, but under the urban reform, no one could rent out property for profit. Everyone paid rent to the government, 10 percent of their income, and after five years they owned the place. So our maid suddenly owned her own room and could read and write.

That is an example of what socialism and revolution were about for the Veltforts and many other vets.

By the late 1960s, many of Veltfort's students had become professors, and they could take over the department that Ted had helped launch.

Ted Veltfort (left) and David Wald working on a hospital generator in Nicaragua, early 1980s. Veltfort private collection

Above: Ted Veltfort in his workshop, 2003. Photo by Richard Bermack

Right: Ted Veltfort, 2000

Cuba was attempting to become more self-sufficient. The Veltforts moved back to the United States, having accomplished what they had set out to do in Cuba. Ted Veltfort eventually became head of the electronics section of the department of surgery for Mount Sinai Medical Center. As could be expected, his house is filled with computer projects: "Science and politics go on in spite of my disappointment in both." He keeps his spirits up by corresponding with people on line. When asked about his proudest scientific accomplishments in Cuba, he responded, "That isn't what sticks out in my mind. It is all the things I learned from the Cuban people, about different cultures and about life."

In 1992 Hilda Roberts joined a caravan sponsored by Pastors for Peace, an interdenominational group that delivers humanitarian aid to Latin America and the Caribbean countries. The group boarded a school bus loaded with computers and medical supplies and headed to Cuba. When their bus was seized by U.S. border guards in Houston, the group refused to leave. Roberts, over seventy years old at the time, went on a twenty-three-day hunger strike, along with the rest of the group. The government finally relented and let them continue on to Cuba.

In 1993, Milt Wolff, Milt Felsen, Nate and Corine Thornton, and Hon Brown, the widow of Archie Brown, went to Cuba with Global Exchange to challenge the U.S. travel blockade. The group delivered medical supplies and a check from VALB to a children's hospital in Havana. The group also met with Cubans who had fought with the international brigades in Spain. When they returned to the United States, their passports were seized. "The last time my passport was taken was in 1939, when I returned from defending the Republic of Spain against fascism," Milt Wolff thundered at reporters after being released by immigration officers.

Nate and Corine had met in 1986 during the fiftieth anniversary celebration of the international brigades in Spain. "I was drawn to Nate's sparkling personality," Corine states.

Nate and Corine Thornton en route to Cuba in 1993, challenging the U.S. travel blockade. Photo by Richard Bermack

As a youth, Corine had been radicalized by three events: viewing photos of the Spanish civil war in the *Kansas City Star,* reading *The Grapes of Wrath,* and hearing her father's chagrin one election day. He had gone to work for the Democratic Party and had been handed a list of polling places where he was to cast ballots. "I learned to question authority," she states. She joined the Communist Party but was expelled in 1950. "I guess I learned to question authority too well. They were too dictatorial and lacked a sense of humor," she muses. Nate never joined the party when he returned from Spain. "I still agree with the philosophy, but I never felt compelled to join," he states.

Now a great-grandmother in her eighties, Corine is passionate about shutting down the U.S. Army's School of the Americas. Every year she travels to Fort Benning, Georgia, for the annual protest. In 2000 she was arrested at the school. The next year she took vet Dave Smith and several VALB associates, including Mike McGraw and June Spero, to Georgia with her. Corine is also a member of Grandmothers for Peace and is a fixture at demonstrations against the Lawrence Livermore National Laboratory.

Vet Sam Walters, a photographer and machine gunner in Spain, made one final journey to Cuba. Always the rebel, in defiance of the United States blockade he had arranged for his body to be buried in Cuba. He died in 2000.

Notes

1. Jimmy Yates, *Mississippi to Madrid: Memoir of a Black American in the Abraham Lincoln Brigade* (Seattle: Open Hand, 1989)
2. *The Volunteer,* Winter 1998
3. Judy Montell, interview with Ruth Davidow, 1997
4. Ibid.
5. Carroll, *Odyssey*
6. Ibid.
7. Lou Dematteis with Chris Vail, *Nicaragua: A Decade of Revolution* (New York: W. W. Norton, 1991)
8. Ibid.
9. Information on vets' activities in Central America is from the author's conversations with Osheroff, Roberts, and Smith, and from 1983 articles by Peter N. Carroll in *The Volunteer.*

AFTERMATH

If I am not for myself who will be for me? But if I'm only for myself then what am I? The time to act is now.—Rabbi Hillel

How does one balance political commitment with survival? People join organizations for spiritual, economic, or social reasons, and for a movement to succeed in the long term, it must address those concerns. In the 1930s, the Progressive movement attracted some of the best and the brightest. Vets who had fought in Spain found doors to this world opening for them. As Milt Wolff states:

The vets put their asses on the line. We had a certain panache and coin of the realm that gave us something with people on the Left and liberals....After the war and the McCarthy era, we [VALB] attracted lefties who had nowhere else to go. We had speakers at our events like Harry Belafonte, Linus Pauling, and Pete Seeger. We had the support of Broadway actors and Hollywood movie stars.

Describing the enduring bond among the vets, Wolff says:

We fought together. We were wounded together. We saw our comrades killed. And when we got back, we couldn't abandon the Spanish resistance and the other international brigaders. We raised a lot of money, comparatively, to help people.

Being blacklisted intensified their bond, and the VALB organization did a remarkable job of taking care of its members.[1]

Many of the vets continued to fight for socialism in their public lives, but in private went into

Below: Arthur Munday, New York, 1997
Right: Gus Schultz, Seattle, 1998

Above: George Cullinen, New York, 1997
Left: Al Koslow, New York, 1997

Bill Van Felix, New York, 1997

John Hovan, New York, 1997

Marion Noble, Oakland, 2001

Jack Shulman, New York, 1997

Syd Harris, Oakland, 1986

Clifton Amsbury at a VALB meeting at Hon
Brown's house, San Francisco, 1998

Delmar Berg, Oakland, 1998

George Sossenko, 1997

Ralph Fasanella, Oakland, 1984

Al Gottlieb, Oakland, 2001

Clarence Kailin, New York, 2001

business and became quite wealthy, often helping out the poorer vets. Bill Sennett, who was a truck driver during the Spanish civil war, set up a successful transportation business when he returned. He used his wealth to contribute to political causes, such as the Democratic Socialists of America.

The labor movement became a refuge for many of the vets. To name just a few: Milt Felsen worked for the Directors Guild of America; Mike Pappas for the Furriers; Manny Lanser for the Garment Workers; and Lou Gordon, who had been expelled from the Communist Party for going to a concert instead of a meeting, became an official of the United Paperworkers Union. As a union official Gordon wrote a column in his union newspaper to educate members about the civil rights and peace movements. Along with the ILWU, his union employed a record number of vets, including Abe Smorodin, Jerry Weinberg, Dave Gordon, Joe Gross, and Eli Sims.

The Legacy

I am a revolutionary. I don't find it a threatening word. It's a nice word, it's a good word. It's an honorable word. And people who are revolutionaries are honorable people. Some of them are our national heroes, like Benjamin Franklin and Thomas Jefferson. Capitalism, the system we live under, is the main thing standing in the way of

Max Shufer, New York, 1997

But What about the Guys in the Lincoln Brigade?

One of the major obstacles in the way of human progress, of human understanding, is cynicism. The cynicism that states that people only act in their own self-interest or what they believe to be their self-interest, that says within every seemingly altruistic act there lurks a dark core of greed or hatred or fear. To make people behave, the cynics say, to make society work, you have to know how to exploit and manipulate that dark core. That's life, the cynics say, that's just the way people are. And you can listen to this for a while and maybe agree up to a point, but then you say, "What about the guys in the Lincoln Brigade?"

Then the cynics will go to work and talk about raw youth and misplaced idealism and what this faction did to that faction. But they won't go away, those guys who shipped out for Spain to fight for other people's freedom. They stand up in history like the one tree on a battlefield not leveled by the bombing, stand up and make you ask, "How did that happen?" They won't go away. If you talk to them or read their accounts what you hear again and again is that they went to Spain because of a belief in what people could be, in how people could live together, and they put their lives on the line for that belief and a lot of them died.

"But they *lost*," say the cynics, not knowing that it is more important that they fought—fought when they didn't have to fight, fought when it brought no public glory in their home towns, fought to put a lie to the cynicism that keeps people in darkness. They won't go away...And in a world run by cynics, in a time when caring about someone you've never met is seen as weakness or treachery, how much strength have we taken from the thought of them, how much pride and comfort to be able to say, "But what about the guys in the Lincoln Brigade?"

—Independent filmmaker John Sayles

human progress. It keeps people divided, it keeps people unequal, it keeps people from resolving their own problems. That is why I don't hesitate to say I'm a revolutionary. Revolutions can be either peaceful or violent. After fighting in two wars, I favor nonviolence.

—*Saul Wellman*[2]

The Spanish civil war volunteers described themselves as fighters against fascism. Though they could not stop fascism in Spain, they became stalwarts of a mass movement that succeeded in curbing corporate power through antitrust legislation and the regulation of industry in the United States. The Lincoln Brigade began as a military combat unit, but the members of VALB would achieve their greatest successes through community organizing, labor organizing, the creation of social programs, and political work and demonstrations.

Milt Wolff, known for his military prowess in the Lincoln Brigade and in the OSS, describes himself as a pacifist. He wrote an autobiographical novel, *Another Hill*, to debunk the myth of heroism in war and the romanticism of Hemingway's *For Whom the Bell Tolls:*[3]

I wanted to show that war should be a last resort, how it causes people to do horrible things, how anything can happen. Someone who looks like Charles Atlas can turn into a coward under fire, and some weakling with spectacles on his nose can turn out to be fearless.

One of Wolff's major activities in VALB was lobbying legislators and State Department officials to pressure Franco's government to stop persecuting dissidents. Wolff's wife, Frieda, was a political aide to Congressman Ron Dellums, and Wolff worked with Dellums and Frieda to introduce House Resolution 1251, to provide veterans' benefits for the Spanish civil war vets. The measure failed, but it was typical of Wolff's efforts to win legitimacy for the Lincoln vets.

Saul Wellman kept asking himself, "How can I be relevant today?" After leaving the Communist Party, he became a printer and a printers' union activist. On retirement, he relaunched his career as an organizer, speaking at over three hundred colleges and political events before his death at age ninety.

Abe Osheroff produced two documentary films about Spain, *Dreams and Nightmares* and *Art in the Struggle for Freedom*. He is active in the Seattle antiwar movement. Almost ninety years old, he still tours college campuses to lecture about the value of a life of activism:

When I lecture, I tell kids I've never been identified with a cause that won or seen a "good fight" that was pure. So they ask me, "If none of your causes have won, why do you still do them?" I tell them that ultimately you are alone with yourself and your values.

For me, I have enjoyed every moment. It has felt like a privilege to serve the movement. No matter what is happening in the world, you can't give

The Wives and Families

Moe Fishman and Sylvia Thompson in the New York VALB office, 2001. Photo by Richard Bermack

The struggle was a way of life for us. It was very satisfying. We had a good union, good benefits, good health care. It provided an adequate life and an opportunity to do the things you thought were important. We took a lot of pride in raising our kids to have good social values.

—Hon Brown

At the time of the Spanish civil war, few women served in combat. The majority of women to serve in Spain were in the medical service. Evelyn Hutchens was a driver. Marion Wachtel Merriman is one of the few women credited as a combatant. Virginia Malbin had a special role as a social worker working with relief agencies.

With the founding of VALB, the roles changed. Many of the wives became active in the organization. Marion Wachtel was the first commander of the Bay Area post, which was founded by Sana Goldblatt, a nurse. In later years, Hon Brown, Sylvia Thompson (widow of Bob Thompson), and Yolanda Hall (wife of Chuck Hall) helped run the San Francisco Bay Area, New York, and Chicago posts, respectively.

Herb Freeman, whose brother Jack was killed in Spain, carries on his brother's memory through his activism in VALB. The children of the vets, including Roby Newman (son of Robert Colodny), Linda Lustig (daughter of Dave Smith), Martha Olson-Jarocki (daughter of Leonard Olson), Yvonne Corbin (daughter of Rudy Corbin), and Joni and Eric Levenson (children of Len Levenson) help to run the organization.

in to it. If it touches you, you have to act, to at least be a naysayer. That is what I get out of life.

Without passion, nothing happens, but passion is a blinding force without critical thinking. It leads people astray. The impassioned mover of history isn't necessarily a historian. I saw trade union organizers that were decent become opportunists, and most of the revolutionaries I knew were better people before they came to power, yet they accomplished things for people that no one else did.

Len Levenson is one of the communist stalwarts. He was in the party until 1991, when a group of dissidents who were trying to reform it were kicked out at a national convention. He had attempted to attend the convention but was denied delegate status. "Here I was. I had been a Spanish civil war vet, and I had been the organizer in charge of the West Side of Manhattan, from 72nd to 125th, and they wouldn't let me in as a delegate," he states with indignation.

When asked if that affected his beliefs, he responds, "No, I still believe in everything I believed in. I'm still a communist. I'm not going to let a few assholes change my beliefs." He continues as a member of the new group, the Committee of Correspondence.

Today

The Spanish civil war took place nearly seventy years ago, and today few of the veterans of that war are still alive. But the basic values they fought for—the rights of everyone to education, health care, food, clothing, and shelter, for the opportunity to have dignified work, and for religious tolerance—are once again under assault. According to the Congressional Budget Office, the disparity in income between the rich and the poor in the United States is the widest it has been since the Depression.[4] The imbalance between corporate power and the power of the populace has created a crisis in democracy. The government is cracking down on basic civil liberties—the passage of the Patriot Act in 2001 is a prime example—while removing regulations and restrictions on corporations and allowing a few corporations to monopolize the media.

"It's obscene, it's contrary to every moral and religious principle. I've never seen anything like it, the wealth these guys are accumulating at the same time people are living in poverty," roars ninety-year-old Dave Smith, the current San Francisco Bay Area VALB post commander. "The greatest fight is going to be to stop this tremendous accumulation of power on the right and their control of the media. They control the information people receive."

If Catholicism, a religion based on love and compassion, could beget the Inquisition in Spain,

West Wing president Martin Sheen marches with Dave Smith and other Lincoln vets against the U.S. war in Iraq, San Francisco, 2003. Photo by Richard Bermack

Len Levenson, 1997

Two Americas

My love affair with the Abraham Lincoln Brigade, and in fact my debt to its veterans, started many years ago, when I was nine years old. It started the day I stood on the frontier of Spain in October of 1951, the year I visited Europe for the first time. My Argentine father, a former communist and still very much a man of the Left—like many of his generation who had *España en el corazón*, Spain in their hearts—my father had sworn that he would never step on Spanish soil until Franco was gone or dead. But we swear many things in life and life makes demands of us that are not always heroic or definitive; life has a way of confronting us with what Primo Levi called the gray zones. My father was working at the time at the United Nations in New York and he had professional business to conduct in Madrid and Barcelona, and so we came to the frontier of the country he had never wanted to visit in his life even though it had been at the center of that life and on his mind ever since its struggle against fascism in the thirties had inspired him and countless millions around the world.

What I remember above all was that frontier. We had been traveling from France and, because the tracks were narrow-gauge on the Spanish side, it was necessary to descend in Irun, I believe it was, and change trains. My father took me by the hand and walked me to the very edge of Spanish territory. He crouched down to my height, so he could look me in the eyes, and told me that this was the place where the Republic had been betrayed. Here, he said, right here, the

weapons that the Republic had paid for had been blocked by the French, with the acquiescence of the English and the Americans. Proclaiming their neutrality, these countries, future allies against Germany, had conspired to starve the Republic, not realizing that they were, in fact, encouraging the appeasing of Hitler and Mussolini.

As soon as the train began chugging south to Madrid, my father told me another story, in hushed, low tones: the story of the International Brigades, and particularly of the Abraham Lincoln Brigade. Or maybe he used the word "batallion." How they had poured into this country to counteract the spread of fascism, the decisive battles they had won, *el Ejército del Ebro* that had crossed the river and beaten the Falangistas....

Though born in Buenos Aires, I was then a little yankee boy who thought of himself as an American, or perhaps it would be more adequate to amend that to read "from the North"—an American from the North. I refused to speak Spanish, sang the "Star-Spangled Banner" with fervor, and swore that New York was the best city in the best country in the world.

Like any little patriot, I was always looking for a reason to justify my love of my adopted homeland. And yet, I was also the son of a father persecuted by McCarthy, a witch hunt that would eventually lead us to abandon the United States a few years later and head for Chile. At nine years of age, I was living an irreconcilable contradiction: the country I considered my own was trying to exile my father and might perhaps even kill him. The fact that

the very United States that was hounding my family and so many of my family's left-wing gringo friends had also produced the Lincoln Brigade was a source of comfort to me and also one of the first profoundly political lessons I received in my life.

It confirmed me in something I knew but could barely articulate at the time: there were two Americas, one personified by the FBI and J. Edgar Hoover and Joe McCarthy, an America that segregated Negroes and meddled in foreign lands, while the other one, the other America, was made up of citizens who were willing to risk their lives for freedom wherever it was threatened, an America that came to be represented more and more in my imagination by the Abraham Lincoln Brigade. That was the America that I could belong to....

The men and women of the Lincoln Brigade could not know that, many years after they had left Madrid, they would rescue a small nine-year-old boy from confusion and push him toward political maturity; they could not have anticipated that their own existence would help him to realize that there was another deeper and more decent America to which he could pledge allegiance....Never underestimate how an exemplary life can persist in the imagination of others, how it can inspire beyond death.

—from a speech by Ariel Dorfman at the April 1999 VALB reunion; later included in Dorfman's *Exorcising Terror: The Incredible, Neverending Trial of Augusto Pinochet* (New York: Seven Stories Press, 2002)

and the high culture of science and European philosophy could beget the Holocaust in Germany, then it is no more surprising that the egalitarian philosophy of communism could produce totalitarianism and Stalinism in the Soviet Union, or that the fight for democracy and freedom could lead to the witch hunts of the McCarthy era in the United States. That is the contradiction of the human condition. The true legacy of the Lincoln vets is their ability to deal with this essential contradiction and continue to struggle for a more just world. Even though the institutions, organizations, and governments the Lincoln vets fought for, both abroad and at home, appeared to forsake the humane goals and just society they envisioned, the vets were able to distinguish between their ideals and the follies of men and women; rather than becoming disillusioned or giving in to those follies, they were able to use the contradictions of humanity in order to make a contribution.

The vets' final victory of the spirit is that they were able to form a community that lasted beyond most of their lifetimes, a prize that few can claim. At the 2004 reunion dinner in Oakland, only a handful were still alive and able to climb onto the stage, but their community filled the house as VALB gave an award to MoveOn.org.

Whatever the political strategy, the vets' message remains the same. As Milt Wolff states:

You have to get in the good fight and stay in it. You have to care about more than making money for yourself. The business of the big fish eating the little fish is self-destructive. What the hell is the point of getting to the top if you haven't helped move people to a better place? Activism is the elixir of life.

Notes
1. Carroll, *Odyssey*
2. Judy Montell, interview with Saul Wellman
3. Milt Wolff, *Another Hill* (Urbana: University of Illinois Press, 1994)
4. CBS.MarketWatch.com, June 1, 2004, "'Inequality Matters' Conference Puts Nations on Alert," by Thomas Kostigen

APPENDIX: A HISTORICAL OVERVIEW

The Spanish civil war is part of the age-old struggle between the haves and the have-nots, of the powerless rising up against those in power. During the Dark Ages, the monarchs of Europe claimed a divine right to rule with absolute power. The common person's purpose in life was to serve God by serving the monarchy. People were born into a rigid class system characterized by religious intolerance, prejudice, and racism. Criticism of authority was equated with blasphemy.

The Dark Ages gave way to the Age of Reason and Enlightenment. A merchant and intellectual class based on trade and the production of goods grew, breaking the grip of the land-based aristocracy and the church. People overthrew their oppressors and replaced the monarchs with democratic republics.

In the Declaration of Independence, American revolutionaries proclaimed that "all men are created equal, that they are endowed by their Creator with certain unalienable Rights, that among these are Life, Liberty and the pursuit of Happiness. That to secure these rights, governments are instituted among Men, deriving their just powers from the consent of the governed." They called for religious freedom and the separation of church and state "to keep forever from these shores the ceaseless strife that has soaked the soil of Europe with blood for centuries," as James Madison put it.

In France, the revolutionary philosophers Voltaire and Rousseau proclaimed the universal rights of all humanity, condemning the rule of the church and advocating tolerance of all people regardless of race or religion. In much of Europe, feudalism was replaced by free enterprise, based on the concept that everyone had an equal opportunity to compete in the marketplace by offering their goods and labor. Those with the most socially useful goods and services would be justly rewarded for their efforts, thus benefiting society as a whole.

Unfortunately, the goal of equality proved to be only theoretical. Power begat power. Businesses grew, forming huge monopolies capable of crushing their competition and controlling the market. The free enterprise system gave way to capitalism. Power and wealth were no longer acquired by producing socially useful goods, but rather by the manipulation and control of capital. The workers who produced society's goods were forced to accept subsistence wages offered by factory owners.

The aristocracy had been bound by the doctrine of noblesse oblige—with their power came a responsibility for the welfare of those they governed. The new ruling class and intellectual elites were divided on this issue. Many felt that they should be free to exploit other people. They used the doctrine of survival of the fittest to justify their social position. Those who starved to death or were forced into near slavery were inherently weak. Life was seen as war, with the victor claiming the spoils. That meant big business over those they employed and those whose services they could buy, including politicians.

New progressive movements rose up to oppose the inequalities that resulted from capitalism. Liberals challenged the conservatives' claim that freedom for all included the right to exploit others, asserting instead that responsibility for the welfare of others is part of being human. They proposed regulations on business, such as antitrust laws to stem the power of monopolies to control the market, and social welfare legislation. Socialists and communists called for society to be run for the common good, not for the benefit of business. They advocated an economy based on cooperation, not competition. "From each according to their ability, to each according to their need," Karl Marx stated, calling for private property to be replaced by common ownership.

World War I devastated Europe, creating worldwide chaos and social unrest. The Russian revolution resulted in a communist government that took over private industries, sending shock waves through business communities everywhere. Communists led an unsuccessful rebellion in Germany, and socialist parties in Europe became powerful enough to vie for power in elections. A growing labor union movement challenged the power of bosses at the work place.

In the United States, President Franklin Delano Roosevelt launched the New Deal, which he described as follows:

The word "Deal" implied that the government itself was going to use affirmative action to bring about its avowed objectives rather than stand by and hope that general economic laws would attain them. The word "New" implied that a new order of things designed to benefit the great mass of our farmers, workers and businessmen would replace the older order of special

privilege...because the American system visual-
ized protection of the individuals against the
misuse of private economic power, the "New
Deal" would insist on curbing such power.[1]

The New Deal attempted to return to the Enlightenment concept of the social contract, that societies are based on a common agreement by their members to abide by certain laws and principles for mutual security. In exchange for abiding by the laws of society and putting in a fair day's work, members of society would be guaranteed relative economic security, food, clothing, shelter, education for their children, and, eventually, health care. Social security and unemployment programs were instituted. Regulations giving workers some minimal rights to fair treatment by employers were implemented. Antitrust regulations stemmed the power of businesses to form monopolies. The first consumer protection laws were passed.

Not surprisingly, big business responded to the reforms as if a shot had been fired across its bow. Instead of making concessions, they cracked down. Big businesses around the world attempted to counter social unrest with fascism. Under fascism, industry, religion, and the state merge, and the power of the military is used to crush any opposition.

For example, the Nazi government took power in Germany in the early 1930s. They arrested union leaders, members of rival political parties, communists, journalists, and any other critics. Books were burnt and freedom of speech was curtailed.

Fascism operates by using propaganda and the media to manipulate people through fear, blaming national problems on minority groups and foreigners. It is based on the worship of power and domination over others, with appeals to racism, nationalism, religious intolerance, and sadism. The fascist government in Germany claimed that the German people were a superior race whose destiny was to purify humanity of lesser races, thus glorifying war and brutality.

The War in Spain

That was the philosophical and political stage on which the Spanish civil war was played out. Industrialists and the old aristocracy, including the church, supported Franco and the fascists, hoping to stem the rising pro-worker movements. Although the Spanish Republic was actually a coalition of diverse groups, ranging from middle class intellectuals to anarchists to communists, Franco's supporters successfully labeled all those who opposed Franco as communists. The loyalists claimed to be defending democracy and freedom against a fascist dictatorship, and Franco's forces claimed to be defending the church against godless communists.

Many of the industrialist elites in the world's democratic countries were sympathetic to the fascist response to labor unrest and the demands for reforms. Major corporations, including Ford and General Motors, offered support to Franco and to Hitler. IBM designed the information technology used to manage Hitler's concentration camps. *Fortune* magazine extolled the virtues of fascism. Marine Corps General Smedley Butler testified to Congress that he was offered millions of dollars by a man who claimed to represent the directors of major corporations, including Goodyear Tire, Anaconda Copper, and Bethlehem Steel, to raise an army to overthrow President Roosevelt and take over the White House.[2]

The United States government's toleration or even encouragement of fascist solutions to the threats to business interests by popular movements would become all too common in the second half of the twentieth century. One of the most grievous examples was the CIA-sponsored coup in Chile. Augusto Pinochet led the violent military coup, overthrowing the democratically elected President Salvador Allende. South America's oldest democracy was replaced with a fascist government characterized by torture and the murder of thousands of it citizens.

In 1999, in a moment of poetic justice, a Spanish judge, Baltasar Garzón, indicted Pinochet for crimes against humanity under international law. In April 2000, Judge Garzón addressed the Lincoln vets at the annual VALB event in New York. To all those present, it was clear that Pinochet was a stand-in for Franco. Garzón hoped that the indictment would put dictators on notice that they are answerable to international law, and

that the world community was taking a stand against fascist dictators. He then went on to acknowledge the contribution of the Lincoln vets. The following is an excerpt from his speech:

"The twentieth century has been the most violent period in human history; it has also been the most humiliating for mankind, to the point of making us question our idea of man as a rational being, in the face of so many disasters and massacres of innocent beings.

"But it is also true that, following each disaster, piece by piece we have assembled a universal structure of ethical conscience that today opens the portal of hope for a better world, with greater solidarity and justice, at least in the face of the great disasters.

"Those who sixty-three years ago made the decision to be volunteers for liberty, and who [showed] selfless solidarity with the Spanish Republic broken by the fascist coup are also part of this new awakening of justice today.

"The formation of the international brigades was an act that moved the hearts and minds of the entire world in 1936, a tragic year for all Spaniards. For many the [brigades] were a sign of inspiration and hope that finally the world was reacting to the expansion of fascism.

"Today we remember with deep-felt pride those knights of liberty who fought against the evils of international fascism, moved by loyalty to Spanish constitutional democracy and the legitimacy of its republican government. Today the unforgettable Robert Hale Merriman, Oliver Law, Steve Nelson, Leonard Lamb, Al Kaufman, Stephen Daduk, and so many others are with us, in the memories of many; they are and will always be unforgettable, for they gave their lives for an idea, to build a different and better world."

Notes

1. Samuel Rosenman, ed., *The Public Papers and Addresses of Franklin D Roosevelt,* Vol. 2 (New York: Random House, 1938), cited in Joel Bakan, *The Corporation: The Pathological Pursuit of Profit and Power* (New York: Free Press, 2004)

2. Jules Archer, *The Plot to Seize the White House* (New York: Hawthorn Books, 1973)

ABOUT THE AUTHORS

RICHARD BERMACK began photographing veterans of the Abraham Lincoln Brigade in the early 1980s. He also helps produce their quarterly publication, *The Volunteer.* He has a background in radical oral history and documentary photography. He works as a journalist and photographer for labor unions and progressive causes, specializing in social services. He has produced documentary projects on drug addiction, poverty, radical history, union organizing, child welfare, health care reform, and mental health. One of the themes running throughout his work is that value and purpose in life come from community and engaging in the struggle to help other people. He lives in Berkeley, California, with his partner, Nancy Van Zwalenburg. More information about him is available at his website, www.rb68.com.

PETER N. CARROLL is the author of *The Odyssey of the Abraham Lincoln Brigade: Americans in the Spanish Civil War* and several other books. He is chair of the Board of Governors of the Abraham Lincoln Brigade Archives, a nonprofit educational organization. More information about the veterans of the Abraham Lincoln Brigade can be found at their website, www.alba-valb.org.